Do We Hear the Song of This Joy?

Do We Hear the Song of This Joy?

Meditations on the Acts of the Apostles

by Elisabeth Schmidt

Translated by Allen Hackett

The Pilgrim Press · New York

Originally published in French as *Entendons-nous le Chant de Cette Joie? Méditations sur les Actes des Apôtres* by Elisabeth Schmidt; © Les Éditions du Cerf (Paris), 1982.

Biblical quotations, unless otherwise indicated, are from the *Revised Standard Version of the Bible,* copyright 1946, 1952 and © 1971 by the Division of Christian Education, National Council of Churches, and are used by permission. Excerpts marked KJV are from the *King James Version.* Scriptural references marked NEB are from *The New English Bible,* © The Delegates of the Oxford University Press and the Syndics of the Cambridge University Press, 1961, 1970 and reprinted by permission. Quotations marked TOB are from *Traduction Oecuménique de la Bible,* Les Éditions du Cerf and Les Bergers et les Mages, Paris, 1975.

Library of Congress Cataloging in Publication Data

Schmidt, Elisabeth, 1908-
Do we hear the song of this joy?

Translation of: Entondons-nous le chant de cette joie?
Includes bibliographical references.
1. Bible. N.T. Acts—Meditations. I. Title.
BS2625.4.S3513 1983 226'.606 83-13091
ISBN 0-8298-0680-6 (pbk.)

The Pilgrim Press, 132 West 31 Street, New York, NY 10001

CONTENTS

PREFACE

Few people have any questions about how widely the books of the Bible have been studied in every period of history—more than any other literary or historical text.

Throughout my studies and my life I have felt greatly indebted to the specialists—linguists, historians, exegetes, theologians—who have devoted their knowledge and their labor to the service of the Old Testament and the New Testament.

During the last twenty years the book of the Acts of the Apostles has aroused the interest of exegetes, who were doubtless drawn to it by the charismatic movement and by the research of churches in quest of a greater faithfulness to Jesus Christ and to his message. But the book of Acts has scarcely been—at least in French—a subject of meditations accessible to everybody.

Without weighing down the text with learned references, I have tried to help the reader discover, as though for the first time, the stories concerning the birth of the church of Jesus Christ and to rediscover—particularly the person who knows only several fragments of Acts—how this epic of faith unfolds. Thus the purpose of this book is to stimulate the reader's personal reflections.

I know God speaks in the present tense when addressing us in the secret places of our hearts. We cannot foresee—for ourselves or for anybody else—what God wants to tell us.

PREFACE

It goes without saying that to follow these meditations and refer to the passages under consideration, the reader should have a copy of Acts close at hand.

I consider that the author of Acts is also the author of the third Gospel—Luke.

This study is limited to the first fifteen chapters of Acts, those that bring us precious echoes of the first Christian communities up to a decisive point in their history. The later part of Acts relates the voyages of the apostle Paul; these chapters require quite a different rhythm of study.

Elisabeth Schmidt

TRANSLATOR'S PREFACE

In what sense is *Do We Hear the Song of This Joy?* a book of meditations and in what sense is it a study book? The nineteen chapters are tales of the early church, vividly retold with luminous character sketches. Each chapter contains an arresting question that moves one to look deeply into one's own heart and to reassess the faithfulness of one's Christian community. I can picture this book's being used for Bible study in small groups, and I know it can furnish the thought component of home worship. But how and why was it written?

When, in her preface, Elisabeth Schmidt asks us to approach the book of Acts as though for the first time, she is actually retracing her own pilgrimage. As readers of her autobiography (*When God Calls a Woman,* The Pilgrim Press, 1981) will remember, she was brought up by turn-of-the-century atheistic parents and fought her way to a knowledge of the Bible, helped by Suzanne de Dietrich and the Student Christian Movement in its heyday and by the biblical scholars of the Geneva seminary. In her four varied parishes Pastor Elisabeth Schmidt set great store by confirmation instruction, with its stress on the Bible. Not only as the basis of her preaching, but as the standard on which she based her personal decisions, Elisabeth Schmidt has lived by the Bible. Her French publishers put it this way in introducing the present book to their wide readership:

TRANSLATOR'S PREFACE

In her previous books, Elisabeth Schmidt has given evidence of the strength of her faith and of the generosity of her engagement in the service of her brothers [and sisters]. She shares with us, in this new book, the secret of her Christian vitality: her constant and loving meditation on the Holy Scriptures.

I have added a few pages of notes to the translation, principally to link this book with Elisabeth Schmidt's autobiography.

I will not keep you longer from listening for "the song of this joy."

Allen Hackett
East Falmouth, Massachusetts

Do We Hear the Song of This Joy?

I

With One Accord

(ACTS 1:12-14)

All these with one accord devoted themselves to prayer, together with the women and Mary the mother of Jesus, and with his brothers [*1:14*].

Then they returned to Jerusalem from the mount called Olivet [*1:12*].

I picture them as silent during their walk. The apostles, companions of Jesus on the roads of Galilee and Judea, have just lived through the rout of Good Friday, the revelation of Easter, and (so far as they knew) their Master's final disappearance from their eyes. They have just been asked: "Men of Galilee, why do you stand looking into heaven? [1:11]."

The apostles cannot engulf themselves nostalgically in their memories. The risen Christ has clearly commanded them: "Tarry ye in the city of Jerusalem, until ye be endued with power from on high [Luke 24:49, KJV]." This is the realization of a promise repeated several times by Jesus: "You shall receive power when the Holy Spirit has come upon you [1:8]."

As they reenter Jerusalem, will they see any reminders of the events they have witnessed? Big cities, where the important facts of history germinate and burst forth, apparently go right on living in their habitual rhythm.

Nothing is harder for our human nature than to live in uncertainty for the morrow. Humble and daily tasks often become for us the warp on which our anxious days are woven.

We know nothing about what daily life was like for the disciples of Christ before the Holy Spirit was given to them. The only reality that seems important to the author of Acts is the zeal with which the group of the faithful came together for common prayer. Without these gatherings for prayer their lives would have been almost intolerable.

In an upper room—perhaps the one that had gathered the apostles for the last Passover—the first disciples of the Risen Lord found a kind of posthouse on the road of obedience and waiting. It was a place of spiritual refreshment, where their strength was renewed and they found a peace that dispelled all anguish.

We ought never to forget the first picture given to us of this initial nucleus that will be the church: a humble group, impoverished, tense, hanging on a promise of the Lord.

The Gospel of Luke preserves for us Jesus' appeal for

unwavering prayer. Alone among the four Gospels, Luke has kept two parables that teach us, in a paradoxical way, that we must not tire of crying out to God (Luke 11:5-9; 18:1-8).

The text does not provide a complete list of those who took part in these meetings. The eleven apostles are named; silence envelops the tragedy of the absent one. We also learn that Jesus' brothers and *several women* joined them. This no doubt refers to the group of women who followed Jesus from the time of Galilee on, keeping their distance but *with his intimates*. They were the ones who watched at the cross (Luke 23:49). In the next chapter of his Gospel, Luke gives us the names of some who came to the tomb, bringing the spices they had prepared (Luke 24:10): Mary Magdalene, Joanna, and Mary the mother of James. Here, in Acts 1:14, only one woman is named among the group of women and she is mentioned after the apostles: Mary, the mother of Jesus.

Luke insists not only on the group's faithfulness in prayer, but also on its unanimity. Was this easily obtained? Among the gathered disciples no two had lived through the last events in the same way. This was true not only because of their personal characters, but also because they had taken divergent attitudes when Jesus was condemned.

To arrive at unanimity in prayer they had to keep from passing judgment on one another. That was possible only because they had discovered they were all forgiven by God, even as Peter had been, weeping after his triple denial, with Jesus' eyes resting on him.

And as for Mary?

The grief of a mother stirs compassion; friends weep with her at least when it is a matter of death from sickness or war. Luke, telling of the miracle Jesus performed at Nain, notes that a considerable crowd from the city accompanied a widow whose only son was to be buried (Luke 7:12).

But Mary's son had been declared a blasphemer by the religious authorities of his people; had been judged seditious, an agitator against the public order; had been condemned to the disgraceful torture of the cross by the political powers. Under these circumstances friends do not compromise themselves; they keep their distance. Mary had lived through this trial in silence. For a mother, evil inflicted on her child is heavier to bear than evil inflicted on herself.

The Gospel according to John supplies the inscription Pilate ordered placed over the cross in Hebrew, Latin, and Greek: "Jesus of Nazareth, the King of the Jews" (John 19:19-22). Out of diplomacy the high priests demanded that the inscription be changed. Pilate refused. In the eyes of Rome, Jesus was a revolutionary, a condemned political criminal.

For almost two thousand years how much torture has there been? How many political condemnations and executions? Even today, how many mothers are in anguish because their children have disappeared, officially condemned for political reasons? Mary, the mother of Jesus, was one of these women.

How could she have forgotten the denial, the desertions of one or another, despite the filial affection of some of them? But her appearance later among the apostles, joining them in an earnest and unanimous prayer, proves that she had forgiven them, even as Christ had done.

The young woman of Nazareth had meekly accepted her destiny, saying that "he who is mighty has done great things for me, and holy is his name [Luke 1:49]." Here are the last "great things" that "he who is mighty" had done for her: God had given her this serene victory over suffering, the strength of forgiveness that renews love, allowing her to join humbly in the faithful and unanimous prayer of her son's disciples.

This vision of Mary is the last the book of Acts gives us. From here on, so far as Luke is concerned, Mary enters a total and silent oblivion, while the Holy Spirit quickens and spreads the church.

II

Peter Fills Out the Twelve

(ACTS 1:15-26)

His office let another take [*1:20*].

Midway through the first chapter Luke relates the first manifestation of Peter's authority over Jesus' followers. About one hundred twenty of them are gathered. Peter gets up and proposes that Judas be replaced in the apostolic college. It is not known whether or not this initiative was taken after consultation with the eleven.

Why does Peter want another disciple to be chosen when the promise of the gift of the Holy Spirit has not yet been fulfilled? Is it a case of Simon Peter's impulsiveness, with which the Gospels have made us so familiar? Perhaps.

Every political regime abandons those whom it considers traitors to the vindictiveness of the masses. Here it seems that Peter wanted to blot out the memory of Judas by putting another in his place. His plan did not succeed! Judas' kiss in Gethsemane and the betrayal price of thirty pieces of silver are more vividly remembered in the common culture than the parables Jesus taught. All across the centuries Judas' personality has intrigued and troubled the followers of Jesus.

Is the apostle Peter thinking that by this means calm can be restored to those who might have been unnerved by Judas' violent death?

Peter refers to the scriptures. Interpreting texts from the book of Psalms, he finds the announcement—and one might say the explanation—of Judas' betrayal and the necessity for replacing the betrayer. In giving us this information the author of Acts hints at the sharp grief the apostles felt when they called to remembrance the "guide to those who arrested Jesus. For he was numbered among us [1:16-17]."

The first question to arise is this: "*Whom* shall we choose to take the place of Judas?" Peter refuses to make this choice on his own authority. Nor does he ask the other apostles to make it with him. He seems to refuse what might be called co-opting someone but does lay down some of the conditions for the choice.

Among the gathered faithful some had known Christ's message for only a short time. Others still knew too little of his life and teaching. Only those who had followed Jesus from the beginning of his ministry to the resurrection could be joined to the eleven in serving as witnesses of the resurrection.

These conditions are full of wisdom and no one seems to have refuted them. But they limit to two the number of those eligible: Justus and Matthias.

That figure is a solemn reminder. It reveals the slender number of those faithful disciples who had not along the way abandoned the one who was tortured on Golgotha. We ought not to forget this slight number when we come to discover how the gospel is going to spread.

Next to be decided is how the choice will be expressed. No popular movement is seen here, no lifting one or the other into the place of an apostle. In the first century in Jerusalem the kind of popular chorus that will raise Ambrose to the bishop's chair in Milan in the fourth century is not in evidence.

Limiting the number of candidates who could be chosen was easier than limiting the number of those who would do the choosing. But in the context of that time no one would have dreamed of an "election" in the democratic sense. What an impasse Peter had involved himself in! He then resorts to an old Jewish custom. The term drawing lots does not do it justice. It was luck that came into play when the Roman soldiers who were guarding the men on crosses cast lots for Jesus' garments (Luke 23:34). The Jews, however, believed that God's will could express itself in this way when the land of Canaan was divided among the twelve tribes (Joshua 14; Numbers 26).

Before the drawing of lots the short prayer (1:24-25) expresses the embarrassment everyone feels as a result of Peter's proposal. Although the apostles were not conscious of it, this type of prayer seeks to put God at the service of a human project. It is not the prayer of those who are seeking God's purpose.

Matthias was designated. The New Testament never mentions his name again. Thus nothing is known about him. Some traditions attribute an apocryphal gospel to him. Nor will the question of drawing lots come up again.

But the book of Acts speaks to us at length of another apostle—Saul of Tarsus. He himself liked to recall that he was an apostle "not by human appointment or human commission, but by commission from Jesus Christ and from God the Father [Gal. 1:1, NEB]." James, Peter, and John did not immediately give Saul their hands in recognition of his ministry.

Peter was in a hurry to choose this substitute apostle and the man so hastily chosen was soon forgotten. But God, in sovereign liberty, chose a thirteenth apostle, calling him in a way that overturns all the reasonings and wisdom of God's servants—including Peter.

The pious copyist of the old manuscripts may have wanted to suppress this passage, because it contributes little to one's edification. Happily, it has been kept for us, and we find in it the subject of salutary reflections.

We discover that the first group of believers, gathering in Jesus' name, must have asked themselves the question of how to choose their leaders. The same problem will emerge all through Christianity, with different solutions being found in the diverse churches.

Whatever the response given, whether by a hierarchal method or a democratic election by the people of God, if the Holy Spirit does not inspire and enlighten the leaders of the churches, the churches come to resemble the governments of any human society.

How many wise or rational conditions have been imposed for recognizing a call as truly from God. We must also recognize how many judgments have fallen like a guillotine on the fervor of authentic vocations, how many sclerotic organizations close the horizon and no longer have any vision for the future.[1]

Whoever we may be, in the service of God and humankind, the end of chapter 1 brings us back to true humility, the humility which recognizes that God calls and acts well beyond our familiar horizons and in ways we cannot foresee.

Only this humility frees us from all sectarianism.

III

In Our Own Tongue

(ACTS 2:1-13)

Disconcerted, marveling, they said, . . . "How does it come about that each one of us hears them in our native tongue?" [*2:7-8,* TOB].

Seven weeks after Passover the Israelites celebrated the festival of Pentecost. Beginning as an agricultural feast, it had become a commemoration of the gift of the law at Mount Sinai. Many pilgrims came to Jerusalem from all of Palestine and from the nearby territories.

On this day a rumor was going about in the narrow and bustling streets of the city. In one house where a company of believers had gathered "the rush of a mighty wind" was heard. Tongues of fire rested on each one of them.

For pious Jews, such signs called to mind the thunderings and lightnings that made known the presence of God to the people gathered at the foot of the mountain (Exodus 19—20).

Then a crowd moved toward the house.

They all realized that the believers they found there had been shaken by a great emotion and were possessed by an exaltation that took a strange form of expression. The text tells us, in simple words, the secret of all these manifestations: "They were all filled with the Holy Spirit [2:4]."

We can hardly imagine what those ten days were like—the days that had elapsed since their Master disappeared from their eyes. Much less can we have a conception of their inner tension during the silence of waiting. Nor can we readily comprehend the fullness of the joy that invades them when the promise of the Holy Spirit is realized.

Today we are familiar with the fact that our bodies react to all great emotions, including the spiritual. Doctors and psychologists have studied such responses. Perhaps we have been the confidants of persons undergoing decisive religious experiences. We may then have witnessed marked physical aftereffects from spiritual causes.

Here in Jerusalem, on the day of Pentecost, those who remain merely spectators are perplexed, disoriented. Some of them quickly come up with a simplistic and materialistic explanation: "They are filled with new wine [2:12]." These scoffers could not possibly guess that some future Christians would turn their taunt around. Christians would use this figure of speech to express the tumultuous joy of discovering the love of God. The great mystics would speak of being "God-intoxicated."

Most of the onlookers, although uncertain, were listening. Then they heard the proclamation of "the wonderful works of God." These Jews knew the poetry of the psalms that tell of God's miracles and of God's greatness (Psalms 96:3; 105; etc.). No doubt they had often taken part in these prayers in the synagogues or at the Jerusalem temple. But when the Holy Spirit is there the words of the Word of God are as new, as though heard for the first time. No one can explain what takes place in the inner depths of the heart. We can only take note of the bearing of those in whom the Spirit dwells.

I am particularly impressed by two manifestations of the work of the Holy Spirit at the time of this first Christian Pentecost:

To begin with, the first Christian community, which has received the gift of the Spirit, *sings out* the wonders of God. Not a great deal is known about the lives of these men and women, of their ties of family and affection, of their physical and moral sufferings. But should we regret it?

The crucial point is this: In this privileged moment the only thing essential to these people is that God has filled their hearts with an immense joy. Little people for the most part, without influence and ambition, they affirm with extraordinary conviction that God does great things.

Luke, so attentive to the teaching of Jesus concerning the poor and the humiliated, knew how to hear this joy that sings and acclaims God. It is in Luke's Gospel that we find the canticle of Mary—the Magnificat, from the first word of its Latin translation (Luke 1:46-55). And now for almost two thousand years, amid the cries of war and hatred, despite mockeries and persecutions, there have always been Christians to sound forth the songs of praise, whether in private prayer or in the prayer of the community.

Today many complain that the disillusioned sadness of the world has choked out all joy in the churches. These same people groan when they see young people looking for a happiness that the mirages of all sorts of gurus promise them for tomorrow. There are also signs of real hope and joy among the young people. Guitars in church would not have shocked the first Christians.

The second striking evidence of the work of the Holy Spirit in this first Christian Pentecost is that this little Christian community could make itself understood by the pilgrims who came to Jerusalem from the neighboring countries, pilgrims who spoke different languages or dialects.

"Not being understood" is the phrase that expresses the grievance all of us can lodge against one another. Husband and wife complain that "he (or she) does not understand me." So too parents "do not understand" their children—and the reverse. Nations and races lack fundamental understanding of one another.

Particularly in the last few decades of the twentieth century, experts and laypersons have been making many studies of the question: how do people communicate with one another? Even the churches have made a critical examination of their language to avoid speaking only in the idiom of one class, one nation, one civilization (whether Western or Eastern; northern or southern hemisphere; first, second, or third world). Christ must not be a foreigner to anyone. Varied scientific means are at our disposal today so that people may understand one another better. But alas! We frequently have to register failures.

Often common interests or shared ambitions tie people together. These ties appear to be solid but are ephemeral. The Spirit, like a fire, must burn away everything that blocks a true and lasting understanding: our egotism, our pride, the love of money. The Holy Spirit must create in us a joyous love like Christ's love.

IV

My Spirit upon All Flesh

(ACTS 2:13-36)

Here this word of the prophet Joel becomes a reality: . . . "I will spread my Spirit on all flesh" [*2:16-17,* TOB].

Facing the troubling events they had witnessed, everyone was asking, "What does this mean?"

Then Peter stands up to speak. The text allows us to guess that he does it with authority but not with the imperiousness of an officeholder or the dogmatism of a doctor of the law. He is no longer the man who denied his Master at the dawn of Good Friday, while he was warming himself at a brazier in the courtyard of the high priest. The power of the Spirit has made of him a solid man, who lives up to his name Peter, the Rock. He draws himself up to his full height and for the first time addresses the varied folk who have gathered.

Immediately Peter cuts short any explanation of these bewildering events as due to drunkenness or magic. Vigorously, he avoids letting attention stray to nonessentials. He interprets by scripture alone what has just taken place.

The apostle quotes the prophet Joel, in whose writings we find a double current of thought. Living as he did at the return from the exile, Joel sometimes expressed a vengeful nationalism, at the same time affirming the universalism of the revelation that had been given to the chosen people. Peter quotes God's extraordinary promise as proclaimed by Joel: "I will pour out my spirit on all flesh [Joel 2:28]."

The world that was known by the apostles and those who heard them was limited. In the course of generations and centuries others than they will discover farther shores, new continents, and the immensity of the heavenly spaces. Peter proclaims what the prophet had announced: The promises of God are for all people, a concept that will become almost unimaginably vast but that was mind-boggling even in Peter's time. Can we truly assess how insane such words sounded on the lips of an uneducated man in the midst of a little group in a small district in Jerusalem? The Word attested by the Spirit opened out on an immense horizon—the whole of humanity.

Peter does not stop with this first prophecy of Joel but goes on to quote the next few verses: "Yea, and on my menservants and my maidservants in those days I will pour out my Spirit [2:18]." These words call to mind the structures of rural life. Today we would say "the hired help, the workers." "Sons and daughters, menservants and maidservants" were, in the time of Joel and in the time of Peter, the downtrodden, the nobodies. To proclaim that these "little ones" could prophesy was to recognize that these voiceless people had the right to speak with authority if, in a privileged moment, they had been inspired by the Spirit. Theirs would be the authority conferred by God, an authority that leaps over all barriers between social classes and between sexes.

The apostle proclaims that what these men and women are witnessing on this day is the realization of what had been proclaimed by the prophet Joel. The chosen people had sometimes refused the messages of such men of God, whether by attacking them, like Jeremiah, or ridiculing them, like Amos. But the writings of these prophets, still preserved, were heeded.

Before speaking of Jesus of Nazareth, Peter starts from the Word. Then he announces the Christ, his death and his resurrection. Peter quotes anew a certain number of texts from the Old Testament, particularly from the psalms. To the apostle, these verses clearly designate the Messiah descended from David and point to the suffering, death, and elevation of Jesus.

This first sermon by Peter shows us how much continuity there is for him (as for the other apostles) between the scripture of the people of Israel and the teaching of Christ. Their Master had repeated several times that he came "to fulfill the law and the prophets." In the synagogue at Nazareth, Jesus read this passage from Isaiah: "The Spirit of the Lord is upon me, because he has anointed me to preach good news to the poor. He has sent me to proclaim release to the captives." After the reading Jesus said, "Today this scripture has been fulfilled in your hearing" (Luke 4:17-30). It was in this town where he had been brought up that Jesus first experienced a display of hostility.

We have seen that Peter leaves aside the narrowly nationalistic and vengeful passages from Joel but quotes the verses in which the winds are blowing prophetically toward the proclamation of Jesus as the Christ and toward the gift of the Spirit.

Jesus had explained to the two travelers on the road to Emmaus the things concerning himself in all the scriptures, beginning with Moses and the prophets. Luke uses an evocative expression when he reports what the two disciples said to each other, that Christ had "opened to us the scriptures [Luke 24:32]." In the same way Peter opens up to his Jewish hearers a totally new way of reading the scriptures, making them signposts pointing to the coming of Christ.

Have we learned this way of reading the Word?

For many Christians today the situation is the reverse of Peter's. Most modern church people know precisely nothing of "the things concerning Christ" as they are found in the Old Testament (to use Luke's expression).

Beginning with Constantine, when the Roman persecutions against the Christians will cease, Jesus of Nazareth will become "the Jesus of the West," torn loose from the tradition of his people. Several texts from the Old Testament—always the same—will be known, because they are imbedded in the liturgies of the church. But they are detached from their roots. These older readings of scripture by the apostles should bring us up short and call us to meditate afresh on the Word of God in its wholeness.

V

Both Lord and Christ

(ACTS 2:36-41)

God has made him both Lord and Christ, this Jesus whom you crucified [2:36].

Peter uses the scriptures as his point of departure in explaining the gift of the Holy Spirit to all who had witnessed its coming. Then he climbs back along the trail of time as he traces out God's design: the coming Messiah proclaimed; his coming, in the person of Christ; his rejection, put to death at the hands of impious men; God's raising him up from the dead.

These verses are dense, summing up all the Christian certitudes we shall find proclaimed all through the book of Acts. It is hard for us to imagine with what power of conviction Peter could proclaim the lordship of Christ. The first person to become aware of Jesus' Messiahship in his lifetime (Mark 8:29), Peter now reaffirmed it as a witness to Jesus' victory over death. His proclamation was fraught with all the emotion of a man overwhelmed by the love Jesus had shown to him in forgiving him.

These words reach to the most secret places in our beings, where the questions necessary to our lives are raised. These are agonizing questions. The question Peter's hearers were asking translates their anguish: "What shall we do?"

The apostle cannot offer the response that priests of other religions would give. The religion of the occupying Romans, for instance, would answer, "Go make sacrifices at a certain shrine to appease the anger of the gods!" Peter knows and those who are listening to him know that the prophets of Israel rose up against pilgrimages and sacrifices. Isaiah had dared to say, "What to me is the multitude of your sacrifices? . . . Bring no more vain offerings" (Isaiah 1:11-13). Peter does not reply by making moralistic demands. Nor does he suggest a specific action that could be undertaken, like a penance to be paid. His answer is short: "Repent, and be baptized every one of you in the name of Jesus Christ for the forgiveness of your sins [2:38]."

What does the word repent mean? For many of our contemporaries its meaning is vague or does not make sense. Others find their teeth set on edge because the word repent has too often been used in narrowly pietistic circles, where humanity is judged in two classes: the converted and all others. Thus we must strip this word of the garments with which it has been clothed in accordance with different periods and different theological schools.

It is scripture alone that gives the word its meaning. To repent is to turn around, to change direction on the road on which we have set out.

The prophets have put in poetic language God's call for our return. God does not ask us to busy ourselves with performing religious rites or to enter an ecclesiastical system but asks us as free people to find once more the road that leads to the living God who is calling us.

God calls us to life. "I have no pleasure in the death of the wicked, but that the wicked turn from his way and live [Ezek. 33:11]." The passionate breath that animates the prophetic texts shows God with quite a different face from the one other cults reveal—the face of a God who loves and is ready to forgive: "Seek the Lord while he may be found, call upon him while he is near; let the wicked forsake his way, and the unrighteous man his thoughts; let him return to the Lord, that he may have mercy on him, and to our God, for he will abundantly pardon [Isa. 55:6-7]."

Peter's listeners gave to the order "Repent!" the meaning the leaders of the people of Israel had given it in their teaching. Using the texts of the psalms, they had certainly sung of God's mercy during their celebrations in synagogue or temple.

Luke has kept for us the parable wrongly called the prodigal son (Luke 15:21-32). This son, whose misery is leading him to repentance, takes the road back to his father. His father welcomes him, opening his arms to him. This parable will inspire the extraordinary painting by Rembrandt, in which the father's hands are luminous as he presses to his breast the son who has been found again. This parable will say to all people on the Mediterranean shores and then to other continents what is the secret of the love of God.

But after the first Pentecost, in the heart of old Jerusalem, Peter draws up before his coreligionists a new indictment. He does not enumerate the sins so often named by the prophets. Some One makes them visible; it is Jesus placed on the cross, the sight of whom is unbearable.

Is there not in this indictment proclaimed by Peter a kind of disconcerting brutality, too compressed a résumé of the Christian faith, that is so hard for us to understand? Could those who first heard this sermon accept Peter's verdict? In saying "this Jesus whom *you* crucified" (italics added) Peter holds them personally responsible. But not every hearer had been among those who cried to Pilate, "Crucify, crucify him! [Luke 23:21]." With all the stronger reason the twentieth-century Westerner reading these words may be able to consider that he or she is in no way guilty of this death.

It has always been tempting to load on the Jewish people alone the responsibility for the death of Jesus. Some theologians have even called the Jewish people deicides. Some Christians who claim to be followers of him who died praying, "Father, forgive them, for they know not what they do," have despised, persecuted, exterminated Jews. This tragedy has occurred in many different epochs—and still goes on today.

Nevertheless—for it will soon be twenty centuries—men and women have pondered, meditated before the story of Jesus of Nazareth. At the end of the road of his obedience we see this cross set up on a little mound, where he died saying,

"It is accomplished [John 19:30, NEB]." This cross reveals many things that are hidden.

We find ourselves so much like those who rejected Christ and so mysteriously at one with them. We crucify him afresh by our love of money, our love of political power, our collective cowardice, our contempt for the "little people." It is always the same—always.

At the same time the cross reveals our condemnation it teaches us the forgiveness of the One who loves us.

We can benefit from all the admirable pages of meditations recorded by so many Christians. We can listen to the music of so many liturgies or to the passions of Johann Sebastian Bach.

All these testimonies bring alive the short, rough word of Peter: "God has made him both Lord and Christ, this Jesus whom you crucified."

VI

The Song of This Joy

(ACTS 2:42-47; 4:32-35)

And they, continuing daily with one accord in the temple, and breaking bread from house to house, did eat their meat with gladness and singleness of heart [2:46, KJV].

We have in these several verses a quick but compact picture of what the life of the first Christian community was like. Luke speaks of the members who composed the community, not calling them friends (a title his Greek culture would have made familiar to him) but believers. One common faith is certainly the essential and deep link that binds them together and expresses itself in their whole bearing toward one another.

The unity of this community is underlined twice in this

brief passage (2:44, 46). This closeness impressed contemporaries and continues to strike the readers of the New Testament. Actually, these five verses, often considered, have been pulled out of context to be brandished as a new decalogue in order to judge our old churches. Again, they have been used by political ideologues. Would that we might have the grace to read these lines as if we were doing it for the first time and to hear in them a message that is always contemporary.

It is astonishing to see the spontaneity of this communion that is not in the least concerned with any kind of organization. They were all living out, around the apostles, the experience Christ had promised: "Where two or three are gathered in my name, there am I in the midst of them [Matt. 18:20]."

These believers continued to go to the temple faithfully each day. It seems that they did not see any contradiction between their faith as Israelites and the fact of eagerly learning another teaching—that given by the apostles. The time for ruptures had not yet come. Our Western minds, clad in the armor of juridical and Cartesian notions, ask for a neater cutoff from the Jewish past. But the course of history is not always neat.

This community, seemingly so fragile and showing no rational guarantee of permanence, nevertheless manifests a disconcerting strength. "*With great power* the apostles gave their testimony [4:33, italics added]." What, then, was going on?

Other pages of the book of Acts tell us how the message of Christ was carried beyond the walls of Jerusalem.

But first, the group of three thousand (2:41), which was

growing each day, was living its faith. They gathered to pray, to share their meals, to be taught. Their faith expressed itself in a new spirit in their lives with one another—respectful love acted out in community. Their faith was a wellspring of life to them.

We are accustomed to the discrepancy that exists between the demands of the gospel and the way in which we put them into practice in the concrete situations of our daily lives. These first disciples put into practice immediately and to the very end what they understood in the teaching of the apostles and in the communion of Jesus Christ.

Around A.D. 33—and still today—this first Christian community in Jerusalem had something astounding in the way it bore witness to its faith. There are several aspects of this surprising Christian style.

The community presented a certain socioeconomic diversity: Some of the members owned land or houses; others were "little people" and in need. Thus Luke underlines in chapter 2, and even more insistently in chapter 4, that those who were the richest stripped themselves of their goods and brought them to the community for distribution.

The Hebrew people knew that the land belongs to God and that it is only entrusted to those who are its "proprietors." Jesus had recalled that we will all have to give an account of our stewardship before the only true Owner of our goods, God.

But the gesture of those who laid down their belongings at the feet of the apostles struck home. The instinct of property is powerful. The child already knows how to insist: "That's mine!" The adult has the whole apparatus of justice to defend his or her rights. Thus any act of giving up one's goods is a sign that has always made one stop and think. Such an abandonment of prudential ways declares without words that true wealth is elsewhere, not invested in what we call goods.

The act of cutting oneself off from one's possessions has been seen as a repudiation of the established order and of habitual social conventions. It is frightening, while at the same time it shows God's action in a life. But we must be careful: The text does not give us the right to make of these giving gestures an obligation, a constraint, or an entrance requirement for joining the community. These gifts are described as individual, spontaneous initiatives. For example, Peter will say to Ananias, in connection with his field, "While it remained unsold, did it not remain your own?" In other words, "You did not *have* to sell it. Why, then, your deception?" (See Acts 5:1-11.)

The only reason for these gifts is love. The well-to-do believers could not live with the idea of having indigents among them. This unity of the believers would not have been possible if some had lacked necessities, sitting next to those who were rich. When the love of God fills the heart, a love shared with the other believers, the sharing of goods only expresses that love. To know that a brother or sister is in need is a suffering that burns until it becomes possible to assuage it.

Long before Jesus' word "that they may be one [John 17:11]" would be recalled to divided Christians, it was lived out by this community in acts and with plenitude.

Perhaps we are less conscious of another aspect of the

witness of this community: that of its joy and lightsomeness.[1] However, everything is linked. The young man in the parable goes away very sorrowful (Luke 18:18-30), *because* he does not want to let go of any of his possessions. Conversely, wherever giving is practiced, joy reigns—a quality of joy that leaves no bitterness or regret and whose echo remains.

It is the joy of the sharing of faith and hope, the joy of forgiveness. This joy is unintelligible for those who are far from God. But we would have been able to see its luster on the radiant faces of these early Christians and to catch their jubilant song when they came together. Giving is a source of joy as great—or greater—for the giver than for the receiver (Acts 20:35).

The gesture of stripping ourselves of things frees us from so many conventional attitudes connected with wealth. This gesture helps us to live in a climate of truth. I like this expression of the author of Acts in describing the atmosphere that prevailed in the meetings of these believers: They lived all these things "with . . . singleness of heart [2:46, KJV]." These words evoke for us the calm unity of their hearts, sustaining them in their hours of dispersion and as they came together in sharing.

The question for us is "Do *we* hear the song of this joy?"

VII

By the Gate Beautiful

(ACTS 3:1-10)

And Peter directed his gaze at him, with John, and said, "Look at us" [3:4].

What a contrast between the splendor of the temple restored by Herod and the misery of the poor and the sick huddling at its gates! More for his own glory than for that of God, Herod in the year 20 B.C. had already begun the building operations that would almost double the space reserved for the temple and its auxiliary buildings. He had laid foundation walls that would assure its solidity and had bestowed on its doors a sumptuous splendor.

A large crew was in charge of keeping order on the premises. Meanwhile, Roman soldiers, on guard in the Antonia Tower at the northwest, kept the vast Court of the Gentiles under surveillance.

No one is surprised to find that so many beggars are gathered at the temple doors precisely at the time when there is the most coming and going by those who frequent the temple for prayer. The sick and the lame know that as the worshipers draw near to God they cannot help but feel compassion for all these unfortunates. They are expecting that such pity will express itself in alms.

Almsgiving plays a large part in Jewish piety. Many Old Testament texts are concerned with the widow, the orphan, the sick. They suggest that there is nothing small-minded in the person who fears God and shows it by a gesture of generosity. Psalm 112 extols the mental health of the philanthropist:

> It is well with the man who deals generously and
> lends. . . .
> He is not afraid of evil tidings; . . .
> His heart is steady, he will not be afraid. . . .
> He has distributed freely, he has given to the
> poor;
> his righteousness endures for ever.
>
> —Psalm 112:5, 7-9

Jesus enlarges on the practice of almsgiving, which he refers to frequently and has no idea of suppressing. He sees giving alms in a new dimension, as an indicator of a whole personality. Here in Jerusalem, where public benevolence was organized and private charity was large, Jesus admires the widow who "out of her poverty put in all the living that she had" (Luke 21:1-4). He also commends Zacchaeus, who decides to distribute half of his goods and to make restoration for the wrongs he has caused (Luke 19:1-10).

In this third chapter of Acts we see Peter and John going to the temple by the gate Beautiful, the most splendid of the nine gates that opened on the court. It is the one whose vast portal of polished brass needed twenty men to open and close it.

The apostles go as a pair, as their Master commanded (Luke 10:1). Here they are, then, in the presence of beggars and the handicapped seated or lying on the beautiful mosaic of the ground, waiting for an alms.

In the community of believers the apostles have experienced the joy of sharing goods; they have seen the money brought in from the sale of a field or a house and laid at their feet. What are they going to do in this place, where the most traditional form of charity is practiced? Something unforeseen happens. A forty-year-old man crippled from his birth has been brought every day to this gate. On the day Peter and John are near the gate Beautiful this lame man holds out his hand for alms with a gesture that has become mechanical. Instead of feeling a coin he hears a voice saying, "Look at us." It is Peter speaking, with John beside him. The apostles wanted their gaze to cross that of the handicapped man. For them, he is no longer just another beggar to whom one might absently give something. By fixing him with their eyes they were making it clear that, for them, every person is a unique being, a creature made in God's image. Love exacts of us this recognition of the value of the other person.

We are not all like the wicked rich man who never saw poor Lazarus at his door (Luke 16:20). But we do practice a certain cowardice, which makes us run away from the sight of suffering. However great our attachment to money, do we not sometimes use it as a way of exempting ourselves from the need to look at human distresses face to face? We instruct others to do it for us when we give to charitable organizations.

Peter and John are not seeking an exemption. Riveting the lame man with his gaze, Peter says to him, "I have no silver and gold [3:6]." He almost flaunts his poverty here among those who are expecting the traditional gesture. Although Peter's words seemed brusque to the would-be recipients of his charity, they may bring comfort to embarrassed Christians who are poor. They would like to be generous donors but simply cannot be because of their poverty. Peter's words should forever banish such regret.

"I give you what I have." The apostles have something else to give rather than a little money. It is something which cannot be seen or measured. It is something people cannot destroy, as in the year A.D. 70 they will destroy the magnificent portal of the gate Beautiful and the whole temple with it.

There is a teaching of Christ which is hard to understand: "But give for alms those things which are within; and behold, everything is clean for you [Luke 11:41]." This inmost and deepest part of our hearts—it is from there we should draw what we ought to give.

It is the strength of his faith, the love Christ has placed in him that Peter wants to transmit to the unhappy lame man, resigned as he is to his fate. Peter takes him by the right hand, repeating the gesture he has seen his Master use. It is a gesture of tenderness that cancels all distance and contrasts with the solemn invocation, "In the name of Jesus Christ of Nazareth, walk." The apostle wants it clearly understood that the gift of healing comes from Someone other than himself.

We cannot forget that this story is written by Luke, "the beloved physician," as Paul identifies him in Colossians 4:14. Luke is an educated Greek turned Christian and now Paul's companion. In his Gospel, Luke makes a large place for the poor, the lowly, the sick. He describes some of the symptoms of their diseases. The healing of the lame man is not contested by anyone. The members of the Sanhedrin in their deliberations say to one another, "We cannot deny it [4:16]."

In the cultural climate of the time, when the miraculous and the irrational are familiar, the lame man's walking might have passed unnoticed if his healing had not been done in the name of Jesus of Nazareth.

The healed cripple, accompanying the apostles, becomes a sign. He is a sign that the power of God in Jesus Christ repulses the miseries that shackle humanity. He is a sign that those who are resigned to their fate rise up and walk. He is a sign that Jesus strikes hidden springs in the hearts of those he has freed, so these springs pour out songs of joy and praise.

VIII

The Boldness of Peter and John

(ACTS 4:1-22)

Now when they saw the boldness of Peter and John, and perceived that they were uneducated, common men, they wondered [4:13].

From that time on nobody passed in front of the man lame from birth at the gate Beautiful, where, until that time, he had been brought faithfully every day. His sudden healing caused some astonishment; Israelite worshipers ran to see him. And because the man clung tenaciously to Peter and John, the two apostles found themselves surrounded by many people.

Luke shows us in his Gospel and in Acts a pattern for

the spread of the gospel, which will ultimately reach the boundaries of the Roman Empire. We already guess it in the first chapters.

Until then Peter had proclaimed Christ in houses, to the extended group of believers. Here we see him taking a step farther; he preaches inside the vast enclosure that marked off the Court of the Gentiles. In the gallery called the Portico of Solomon, between splendid stone columns covered with carved cedarwood, the apostle speaks to the people who surround him.

Again, he seeks to remove all equivocation, to reject every idea of magic power that might be attributed to the apostles. He proclaims that Jesus is the suffering Messiah announced by the prophets. He hopes to set ringing in their ears the words of Isaiah 53:3, 5 in which the Suffering Servant is described: "A man of sorrows, and acquainted with grief; . . . from whom men hide their faces . . . wounded for our transgressions, . . . bruised for our iniquities." Then Peter calls for conversion, recalling the plan of salvation for all people.

Nothing suggests that there was any tumult or agitation among the crowd during this sermon. Nevertheless, the captain of the temple, who held an important post in the priestly hierarchy, joins the priests in confronting the two apostles. What was the complaint against them? Not that they had disturbed the order of the holy places, but that they had spoken about Jesus, recently condemned, and proclaimed his resurrection. The high priests think it best to put the apostles in some sort of protective custody, awaiting their examination, which was to take place the next day.

Here, then, is the first imprisonment of the apostles. It will be followed by many others in the early days of the church. Then, all down the centuries, how many arrests and trials! And today we do not know the great number of those who, over the whole surface of the earth, are suffering for their faith.

On the morrow Peter and John are dragged from their dark cell and questioned. Let us try to understand the situation as it unfolds, to penetrate the characters and the motivations of those facing each other: the judges and the indicted.

Annas and Caiphas (the same men who judged Jesus) and the higher clergy formed the priestly class. Their honorific posts, often held by the same family, gave these clergy a political power linked with their religious power. They were arrogant, self-serving, and crafty. The historian Josephus tells us that they were on good terms with the privileged, but that the common people disliked them.

On this occasion, as 4:2 notes, we find among the priests the vexation and the jealousy of a clergy that is certain they alone possess the whole truth. Therefore, they cannot bear it that others should trespass on their prerogatives. The accused, facing them, appear as "little people," worthless Galileans.

A first observation troubles the examiners. These humble men, who have no formal education, astonish the priests with their boldness and the freedom with which they express themselves. The priests begin to have second thoughts. Have they underestimated their prisoners? Have they taken fully into account their popularity with the people of Jerusalem? As experienced politicians, they try to find a solution for the insoluble problem posed for them by the healing of the lame man and the preaching of the apostles.

But these great personages of the Jerusalem clergy cannot understand what inspires Peter and John. As though they were dealing with popular agitators spreading a prejudiced propaganda, the priests threaten the apostles, ordering them not to speak of Jesus to anyone (4:18).

At this point the interrogation reverses. Calmly and politely Peter and John ask a question of their judges. They address them not as enemies, but as officials capable of a spiritual judgment: "Whether it is right in the sight of God to listen to you rather than to God, you must judge [4:19]."

These priests knew very well that humans must obey God rather than other humans. They knew the history of their people and remembered that the prophets had been imprisoned when their words displeased kings or religious leaders (Jeremiah 20; 38). However, the question posed by the apostles contains an unacceptable affirmation. Peter and John are saying that it is the will of God for them to speak of Jesus. It follows that the Sanhedrin, in attempting to silence the apostles, is acting contrary to the will of God—an impossible position, especially for priests. We can hardly guess the hidden thoughts of those who heard this question asked of them.

"We cannot but speak . . ."—this answer, given with sober and quiet firmness, commits the future of these followers of Jesus. At the same time it blazes the trail that so many Christians, in their turn, will also take: that of faithful witness, cost what it may.

The scene of this first trial of the apostles shows one

aspect of the gift of the Spirit. The high clergy strikes us as all wrapped up in tradition, constrained by their desire for power, fettered by the wealth connected with their functions.

Facing them, the apostles seem to us free. They are free in the face of the threats that are poured forth. They are free in the face of the chiefs and the rulers of this world. They are free despite their human fears. The Spirit gives us the power to be free—a power that does not come from any of the forces of earth: money, connections, knowledge.

The words "we cannot but speak" evoke the whole paradox of Christian obedience, the reference to another strength than our own, the sign of another realm.

Theologians have written, discussed, and sometimes disputed violently over Christian freedom. We will never explain rationally how obedience to God sets us free. But we are called to live out that freedom in our humble daily duties, as in the gravest hours, the times of crises or persecutions.

IX

The Community at Prayer

(ACTS 4:23-31)

And now, Lord, look upon their threats, and grant to thy servants to speak thy word with all boldness [*4:29*].

Peter and John have just been through heavy hours. They have lived through a night of imprisonment. They have undergone the examination of the Sanhedrin. They have emphatically refused to suppress the name of Jesus.

Once released, they hurry to rejoin their company. The Holy Spirit has gathered them all together in one same faith. They love one another as brothers and sisters. This love manifests itself in their solidarity.

Peter and John are "heard," as the text says simply. They have the attention of the whole group as they tell their

Their prayer is a commitment. For them it cannot be a matter of being content to watch others enter the struggle of faith. Jesus had condemned pious mouthings, vain repetitions that are only words without impact on life (Matthew 6:7).

Their prayer was that "thy servants . . . speak thy word with all boldness [4:29]." The clear implication is that they all knew their weakness and were asking for the self-assurance necessary to overcome it. Luke often uses the word boldness to characterize the attitude of the faithful witnessing to their faith. The Greek word translated as boldness means not only certitude, but even more, freedom in speaking. The witness is freed by the truth that he or she expresses.

Other groups of Christians across the centuries have gone through hours like the ones these verses call to mind. Still today in many countries Christians are threatened and gather clandestinely to pray. They know the chiefs and rulers of this world often "take counsel together, against the Lord [Ps. 2:2]." In the midst of threatening dangers they too persevere in prayer, asking for the strength to bear faithful witness.

Why can our prayers not join with theirs? Let us admit, if we are sincere, that we are afraid of prayers that would commit us.

Another petition follows the first in the prayer of the Jerusalem group in this first century: that healings, signs, and wonders may take place. The three words tend to be mixed together in Acts. In the first century what was behind these expressions? Most likely these words were used to cover everything that defied explanation, everything unforeseen. They pointed to whatever revealed a hidden power.

Even in our scientific era God can insert signs for those who are willing to read them. Were the first Christians aware that the familial affection which ruled among them, their simplicity of heart and their joy, their generosity toward the most humble—all these things would remain through history as "signs"? Did they realize that these natural expressions would be noticed by everybody and counted as the most authentic marks of the ever-living Christ?

X

Prison, Deliverance, and Rods

(ACTS 5:12-42)

But Peter and the apostles answered, "We must obey God rather than men" [5:29].

Perhaps television has helped us to sense the warmth and enthusiasm of oriental crowds, as well as their fickleness. But we still have some trouble picturing the uncertainties, the joys, and the perils in the midst of which the first disciples were tossed about while they lived out their faith with boldness.

In Acts 5 we see first that the apostles enjoy great prestige among the people of Jerusalem and that the group of the faithful is growing.

There is nothing surprising in the behavior noted in 5:15, "They even carried out the sick into the streets . . . [so]

that as Peter came by at least his shadow might fall on some of them." Ignorance, coupled with great misery, is enough to explain such facts. We find the same situation across the centuries and still today. The reports, spread by word of mouth around and outside the city, must have pictured Peter as a magician, a healer of sick bodies and deranged minds. This taste for the miraculous still persists in old Europe. And in our educated society can we not still count an incredible number of clairvoyants and fortune-tellers?

Although converts were added to the community of believers and unfortunates were brought under Peter's healing shadow, there was also a falling away. In chapter 5 we follow the increasing fury of the religious authorities of Israel. Some of the people who had been praising the apostles begin to waver; they are afraid to compromise themselves or to enlist with those on the road to the new faith (5:13).

The apostles are thrown into prison again on the order of the priests, this time so publicly that everyone learns about it. As it turns out, this incarceration throws the high priest into confusion. At night the doors of the prison are mysteriously opened.

Luke knows very well that the deliverance is the work of God. He expresses it by writing that an "angel of the Lord" permitted the prisoners to escape. We can imagine that the guards, won over to the gospel, risked releasing the captives so that as free men they might continue their preaching. Instead of keeping Peter and John in their cell, they sped them on their way, saying, "Go and stand in the temple and speak to the people all the words of this Life [5:20]."

On seeing Peter, John, and their companions freed do

the believers remember another verse of the psalm that sustained their prayer after the first arrest of the two apostles? "The Lord who sits enthroned in heaven laughs them to scorn [Ps. 2:4, NEB]."

The apostles continue their teaching in the temple. They dare to proclaim, "We must obey God rather than men [5:29]." It is an act of defiance.

The Sanhedrin, called into session, sees no other solution than the death penalty for its opponents as the conflict grows between their authority and the propagators of a faith unacceptable to them.

In every period and for all the powerful the death penalty has appeared as a radical solution to all difficulties. But an idea, a message, a faith does not die with those we silence by executing them.

Torn between undying ideas and death threats churches sometimes become timid institutions, submissive to the powerful. They are no longer willing for some of their members to stand up and recall the imperatives of the gospel. The controversial ones are considered unpatriotic, or poor Christians. All this while it is they, the challengers, who are the true friends of the church and the true witnesses of Christ. Sadly, they have to recognize that the church is like the statue in the synagogue, with its eyes blindfolded.

During the Sanhedrin's debate behind closed doors one voice is raised—that of Gamaliel. He speaks with the authority accorded to him because of his learning and the respect with which he is surrounded. Gamaliel is a Pharisee of the liberal tradition, grandson of the geat Dr. Hillel, and a teacher of Saul of Tarsus. There is no evidence showing whether or not he has been touched by the apostles' teaching.

On the occasion Luke records for us Gamaliel states it as a major premise that "we cannot fight against God." Then in his great wisdom he advises the test of time to ascertain "whether this plan or this undertaking [i.e., the apostles' teaching] is of men . . . [or] of God [5:38-39]." In conclusion he warns: "You might even be found opposing God! [5:39]."

Thus Gamaliel procures the release of the apostles. Perhaps the high priest is relieved by this intervention. We can detect a certain uneasiness on his part. He says to Peter and John: "You have filled Jerusalem with your teaching and you intend to bring this man's blood upon us [5:28]." These words are reminiscent of the crowd's reply to Pilate: "His blood be on us and on our children! [Matt. 27:25]."

The apostles are released after being beaten with rods. This was a Jewish punishment. We read in Deuteronomy 25:2: "If the guilty man deserves to be beaten, the judge shall cause him to lie down and be beaten in his presence with a number of stripes in proportion to his offense." These blows were not to exceed forty so as not to wound too grievously. Luke does not tell us the number of blows decided by the Sanhedrin. Not a word is said about the suffering of the apostles. It is great, and the silence in which it is wrapped adds a new dignity to their witness.

Beaten and humiliated like their Master the apostles leave the Sanhedrin, "rejoicing that they were counted worthy to suffer dishonor for the name [5:41]." They are living out the promise of the last Beatitude. "Blessed are you when men revile you and persecute you and utter all kinds of evil against you falsely on my account [Matt. 5:11]."

Wounded in their flesh, they are granted a new respite that they may proclaim the good news of Jesus.

The apostles were the first of a great line of witnesses who have discovered the joy of suffering for Christ,[1] receiving blows without returning them. Shall we one day be among those who share this joy? Peter warns us: "Beloved, do not be surprised at the fiery ordeal which comes upon you to prove you, as though something strange were happening to you. But rejoice in so far as you share Christ's sufferings, that you may also rejoice and be glad when his glory is revealed [1 Pet. 4:12-13]."

XI

New Ministries for New Needs

(ACTS 6:1-7)

As for us, we will continue to devote ourselves to prayer and to the ministry of the Word [6:4, TOB].

Despite hostilities and threats, the number of those who are becoming disciples of Christ is growing. Luke records the conversion of priests (there were thousands of priests in Jerusalem!); these were probably the common priests, a lower clergy, different in status and attitude from the rich and powerful high priests.

At this time, when the community was still limited, "there was not a needy person among them [4:34]." This was because a new and magnificent form of mutual help had been spontaneously created. Large gifts brought to the common treasury allowed a distribution to all, according to the needs of each. But with a community considerably increased, difficulties arise.

We must remember again the large number of poor people in Jerusalem. They could not survive except by public or private charity. The historian Josephus gives us impressive figures on the help distributed in grain and clothing. These relief recipients must have constituted a considerable portion of the faithful in the capital.

Organization succeeds spontaneity, but an organization can be called into question by a fair criticism when the latter is seriously heard. The members of the community took to heart the grievance brought by the Hellenists who complained that their widows were victims of discrimination in the daily distribution of help. The Hellenists' complaint results in a whole restructuring of the community's organization, which in turn means a new way of witnessing.

Neither Peter nor the other apostles are going to make decisions alone. When the general assembly of the faithful has been called together the twelve propose a specialization of tasks. This plan is accepted.

Thus we find clearly stated the specificity of the ministry of the apostles: it is the ministry of the Word linked to that of prayer. They dedicate themselves to it as a priority, and they cannot leave it aside for the responsibility of distributing help.

The Jews heard scripture read in the several synagogues, where the heavy rolls on which it was piously copied were carefully preserved and venerated. The essential and primary character of the ministry of the Word and of prayer is thus publicly recognized in the heart of the city, where a hierarchical clergy continues to practice a ministry of sacrifice in a magnificent temple. The apostles' insistence on preaching and prayer is in keeping with their Jewish origins, although they bring to this ancient office a new content and a new tone.

Who will assume the other service of the church—that of ministering to the needy? Those who will be charged with it are chosen by the plenary assembly and not by the apostles alone.

They will be seven in number, a figure that is not arbitrarily chosen. Seven is, in the tradition of Israel, a number charged with symbolism: the world created in seven days; the seventh, or sabbath day; the year of rest for the land (Leviticus 25:6).

Thus the ordinary disciples are not going to be disenfranchised before the apostles. They participate in the organization of this first church, because they elect seven men who will have great responsibilities. (Certain translations prefer the verb choose above the verb elect, the latter being fraught with political associations.) Then, before everyone, these men are installed in their ministry and receive the laying on of the hands of the apostles after a prayer by the assembly.

The laying on of hands is an old gesture. A father blesses his children (Genesis 48:14). It is a rite of communion when practiced at the time of animal sacrifice. The priest puts his hands on the head of the animal to be sacrificed (Leviticus 1:4). The worshiper who makes the offering belongs to God. It is also a rite of commissioning. Moses commissions Joshua as his successor (Numbers 27:18). Jesus lays his hands on those he blesses and heals. We see throughout the book of Acts a gradual evolution and an enrichment of the meaning of this gesture. It is not limited to the apostles.

Thus the contribution of all the believers to the governance of the community is a further fruit of the God-given Spirit. Such participation ought to remain as one of the marks of the church of Christ.

The names of the seven who were designated have been preserved. They are all Greek names. (How natural that God should inspire diplomatic ways to resolve difficulties.)

Luke, a "fellow worker" of Paul (Philemon 24) at the time of the missions to the gentiles, underlines the fact that Nicolaus, one of the seven, is a proselyte. A proselyte, non-Jew, converted to the faith of Israel who has satisfied the obligatory rites (for example, circumcision) is still not a full-fledged Jew. Nicolaus' designation for an important responsibility in the community shows the spiritual freedom of this still-young assembly.

How will these relief measures be organized? As said earlier, neither the apostles nor the disciples could ignore the organization of Jewish relief in the city. Its structures offered a general pattern to which Christian love will give its own style and tone. Thus in Jerusalem, a city of pilgrimage, the transient poor were helped with bowls of food. Those who lived in the city regularly received provisions and clothing.

Widows are mentioned as being among the beneficiaries of this relief. In the piety of ancient Israel concern for the widow and the orphan has an important place. Perhaps Jesus' attitude toward women has made the disciples more sensitive to the misery—in material things and in morale—the misery in which the social structures of the period kept a large number of widows.

We should like to know in detail the way in which the seven proceed to the distributions, but the vagueness of the text is doubtless intended. The disciples are threatened and have to maintain a certain secrecy. We see that the community still gathers at night (12:6-12).

Despite this reticence in the text we may believe that a worship service was celebrated either before or after the meal taken in their homes (2:46). The faithful had not been able to forget the parable of Jesus: "When you give a dinner or a banquet, do not invite your friends or your brothers or your . . . rich neighbors . . . [but] invite the poor [Luke 14:12-13]."

Did they invite one another when they broke "bread in their homes [and] partook of food with glad and generous hearts [2:46]," poor and rich at the same table? It will be thus at Troas during the evening of the first day of the week, when Paul gathers the disciples in an upper chamber (20:7-11). Doubtless the poor, nourished at a meal, then take home their share of the distribution.

Thus the church, at its beginnings, recognized the necessity of another ministry beside that of the Word and of prayer. Recognizing it, they instituted it. It is the ministry of mutual assistance, practical and familial. Why does the church today not have the same freedom to recognize new forms of witnessing? Why may it not, led by the Holy Spirit, invent new ministries?

XII

Stephen, the First Christian Martyr

(ACTS 6:8-15; 7:54-60)

All who sat in the council saw that his face was like the face of an angel [*6:15*].

The seven had been chosen to organize relief and to oversee its distribution in the Jerusalem community. Stephen, the first named, is presented to us as a man full of faith and inspired. Quickly he reveals himself as active and efficient, winning the confidence of the people.

But the Jews who are opposed to the preaching of Jesus as Messiah intensify their hatred and consolidate their opposition. Their violence is all the sharper because Stephen is a formidable debater in discussions with the members of the synagogues.

These synagogues were numerous—several dozen in Jerusalem. The Jews who had come from different parts of the Roman Empire congregated according to their places of origin, and each group had its own synagogue. At the same time the temple, the place of sacrifice, remained the temple for all. We can imagine Stephen taking part in the worship of one or another of these synagogues and explaining the scripture that had just been read—as every Jew had the right to do—by proclaiming that Jesus of Nazareth is the One who is foretold in the Word.

The most embittered against this new preacher were those of the synagogue of the Freedmen. Its members were descendants of slaves taken by Pompey in 63 B.C. They had been freed, and some of them had become prominent men, admitted to the privilege of being Roman citizens.

While the "little people" are favorable to Stephen, once again the substantial citizens are the ones who draw themselves up against the proclamation of the Crucified One. It is possible that Jews who had come back from the Diaspora had developed a passionate, even fanatical, attachment to the Jewish traditions they had maintained even in the midst of foreign people. But we must not underestimate the reflex of those who feel obliged to defend their acquired positions. Jews who came back to Jerusalem from the Diaspora would probably be both more Jewish and more Roman than the average. This might make them doubly anti-Christian, remembering that Jesus had offended the Jewish authorities and had been condemned by a Roman magistrate.

Coming from Alexandria, Cyrene, and Cilicia (as in the case of Saul of Tarsus, likewise a Roman citizen), these men know how to organize with promptness and violence in order to rid themselves of Stephen. They act like those who are sure of the leverage they can apply.

Bringing Stephen before the Sanhedrin, they accuse him of blasphemy, of having pronounced words against the law and the holy place. But contrary to the accusations brought by the false witnesses at the trial of Jesus, there is no question of Stephen's having opposed obedience to the political power.

"Is this so?" asks the high priest (7:1). Stephen is in full possession of his faculties. At this time no one has yet invented the medico-psychological devices for destroying the personality of a prisoner. Stephen answers the Sanhedrin with pertinent eloquence. He gives his interpretation of the history of Israel, recognizing that Moses has received words of life but that "the Most High does not dwell in houses made with hands [7:48]." Stephen, the accused, ends by drawing up the accusation against the chosen people. He charges that they opposed the prophets and did not recognize the Holy and Righteous One, whom they finally betrayed and assassinated.

In speaking thus before the Sanhedrin, Stephen knows he is signing his own death warrant. His words could be considered blasphemous, and he would deserve death by stoning. Prescribed for eighteen cases, the death penalty by stoning was especially designated for blasphemy (Leviticus 24:16f). When Stephen, filled with the Holy Spirit, says, "Behold, I see the heavens opened, and the Son of man standing at the right hand of God [7:56]," he unclenches a hateful expression of indignation. At the time of Jesus' trial the use of almost identical terms had provoked an immediate reaction from the Sanhedrin: "The whole company of them arose, and brought him before Pilate [Luke 23:1]." What is intolerable to the Jewish clerical hierarchy is the place of Christ next to God.

Then without any formal judgment—for none is indicated in the text—they deal with the disciple as they did with the Master. They set upon Stephen and drag him outside the city to execute him.

Stoning is a long and drawn-out form of torture; the rocks, thrown with hate and contempt, pierce and bruise the flesh. To throw them with more energy, the witnesses take off their garments. On that day a young man named Saul took care of the garments. He was a native of Cilicia and had a married sister living in Jerusalem (23:16).

The torture and death of the first Christian martyr are described soberly. Some touches of this execution have been faithfully handed on.

First, in contrast to the vindictive false witnesses we see Christ's witness, whose face reflects the light of the Risen Lord and whose expression strikes the members of the Sanhedrin. His extraordinary mastery over himself before those who no longer know how to control themselves and grind "their teeth against him [7:54]" and his boldness in proclaiming God's help in the ordeal and in confessing the glory of Jesus Christ bring to groups of Christians an unforgettable encouragement and example.

Two of Stephen's last words have been preserved. Perhaps they were inspired in him by those that Jesus pronounced on the cross. They are almost alike (Luke 23:34, 46). We cannot penetrate to the most secret meaning of such an intimacy with God. We may safely assume, however, that the Jesus whom Stephen had seen in a vision, standing beside God, is also the living Christ dwelling in him and inspiring him at his death.

The prayer "Lord, do not hold this sin against them [7:60]" was his last word. Thus he proclaimed another realm, the one that begins when we live this command of Christ: "Love your enemies, do good to those who hate you, bless those who curse you, pray for those who abuse you [Luke 6:27-28]." Stephen died immediately after proclaiming Jesus as the Messiah. His death sealed his words with authenticity.

So much strength, grandeur, and purity is released from the old text that we can only keep silence before it.

XIII

What Is to Prevent My Being Baptized?

(ACTS 8:5-9, 26-40)

So there was much joy in that city [*8:8*].

[*He*] *went on his way rejoicing* [*8:39*].

After Stephen's death all the members of the community are scattered. Saul is ravaging the church, Luke writes. Up until this time only the apostles had been arrested. Now Saul sends women as well as men to prison. Therefore, the disciples of Christ must leave Jerusalem and take refuge in other regions.

Here, then, are the first refugees for the Christian faith, going from place to place. They have no churches to welcome them. It is a time of testing. It could also be a time of desertions. Not at all! The Pharisee Gamaliel will be able to reassure himself that the tenacity of these exiles comes from God and not from human beings.

The most extraordinary thing is that these persecuted men and women in flight create wellsprings of joy wherever they pass. In the eighth chapter of Acts, Luke, who has already described the joy of the first disciples after Pentecost, perceives other aspects of the reality of this joy.

First, we see Philip, one of the seven, proclaiming the gospel in Samaria and Judea. Thus the program the Risen Lord had announced to the eleven apostles on the slope of the Mount of Olives was beginning to come to pass: "You shall be my witnesses in Jerusalem and in all Judea and Samaria [1:8]."

The Samaritans, heirs of a complex history, were held in contempt by the Jews because of their mixed blood and their syncretism. Jesus had tried to get his contemporaries to give up their judgmental spirit toward the Samaritans. He had gone through Samaria rather than detouring around it (Luke 9:52). The Gospel of John tells us how Jesus had conversed with a woman from Sychar at Jacob's well (John 4:1-42). He had also shown that the Samaritans are capable of gratitude and devotion, like the leper who was healed (Luke 17:15-19). And who does not know of the good Samaritan in the parable (Luke 10:30-37)?

These despised Samaritans, sensitive to signs of deliverance and to miracles, welcomed "the good news about the kingdom of God [8:12]" which Philip proclaimed. Men and women were baptized in the name of Jesus. And Luke writes, "There was much joy in that city [8:8]." This expression surprises us. Up until now Luke has spoken of joy in the community of believers. He thinks of it, in the context of the Christian community, as one of the consequences of faith, one of the fruits of the Spirit. Here, however, the joy seems to have been given to a whole city through the presence of refugees from Jerusalem. But not all Samaritans became baptized converts. Luke does not let us overlook the fact that in this group of believers there was even the first simoniac in the history of the church.

Jesus had said: "No one after lighting a lamp covers it with a vessel, or puts it under a bed, but puts it on a stand, that those who enter may see the light. For nothing is hid that shall not be made manifest, nor anything secret that shall not be known and come to light [Luke 8:16-17]."

This open manner of the disciples, so new in many respects, might have set the Samaritans thinking and begun to offer them some hope. Sometimes an expression of the face or a gesture of solidarity or understanding may be enough to stop the rage of another person or exorcise the demons of hate and vengeance. We are too used to thinking on the mass scale. We deal with organizations that spread over vast territories. Consequently, we tend to forget the importance of the changes accomplished by a single individual. Nevertheless Christ's teaching about light has been proven true in life experiences.

Still today we see villages whose climates change through the presence of couples or individual Christians living their faith. They are like lights shining for everyone. One Christian, looking at an evil to which we have become accustomed, can be the decisive factor in undertaking a way to bring help. This is the way most major welfare organizations and movements have been born. Among the best known, some with international and nonconfessional stature, have even forgotten their roots.

Some time after his successful Samaritan mission Philip also comes south to Judea, inspired by a vision. There he meets an Ethiopian, a high official in the entourage of the queen. This man, despite his important post, appears unsatisfied. He is a man on a quest. This we know from the fact of his making a pilgrimage to Jerusalem. He had even provided himself with a manuscript of the book of the prophet Isaiah. On his way home he was reading from its fifty-third chapter. As he read he pondered as to who had "borne our griefs and carried our sorrows [Isa. 53:4]."

Certainly attracted by Jewish monotheism and meditating on the scripture, he was prepared to receive the message of the Christ of the passion. When Philip had explained to him the significance of the text the Ethiopian immediately asked, "What is to prevent my being baptized? [8:36]." (This is a formula often repeated in ancient baptismal liturgies.)

The answer given is important. Nothing prevented Philip from performing this baptism: neither the fact that his convert was a non-Jew and therefore a pagan, nor the fact of his having brown skin. (The word Ethiopia comes from a root meaning brown, burned.) Here, then, is the first Christian from Ethiopia. Philip had made an innovation well before the question of the baptism of pagans was raised in theory.

We are astonished by the promptness with which the queen's minister asked for baptism. The old texts are not slowed down by psychological descriptions; they are content to tell the facts. We can compare this quick conversion with the gesture of a thirsty traveler looking for water in the desert. Finding a spring, he dashes headlong to drink from it.

Jesus had said, "Ask, and it will be given you; seek, and you will find; knock, and it will be opened to you [Luke 11:9]." What words are there to tell the abundance of joy that fills those who, having searched, have also found?

The secretary of the treasury continues on his way, toward his human responsibilities and cares, mysteriously accompanied by the invisible and abiding presence of Christ. Philip, who has opened the scripture to him, has left him; it is not to Philip, the disciple and messenger, that the new convert clings, but to Christ. The great financier has become a new man, discovering true riches, and Luke is able to write that he "went on his way rejoicing [8:39]."

What an admirable catechist Philip was! He should remain our model. He also knew how to realize the Word in the sacrament. He followed the lesson of his Master, who on the road to Emmaus first opened the scripture to his searching believers and then brought it alive in breaking bread with them (Luke 24:13ff.).

The persecution that forced the disciples of Christ to leave the walls of Jerusalem allowed some of the despised Samaritans, along with a pagan from another country, to receive baptism in the name of Jesus.

XIV

The Conversion of Saul

(ACTS 9:1-30)

I am Jesus, whom you are persecuting [*9:5*].

We had our first glimpse of Saul at the end of chapter 7 of the book of Acts. Then he was one of a group of Cilician Jews who opposed the Christian preaching. He, the scholar—a pupil of the liberal Gamaliel—had not hesitated to become the instrument of a manhunt in Jerusalem. He had asked the high priest for the necessary papers to pursue the disciples of Jesus in other cities.

A man of character, passionately convinced of the truth and of the excellence of his faith as a Pharisee—this is the way Saul first appears to us. Nothing in his behavior suggests an unsatisfied man, a man on a quest.

Can we imagine that he was impressed by the serene

death of Stephen, which he had witnessed? I do not think so; nothing makes us so blind as religious or political fanaticism.

While Saul and his companions are following the Roman road leading to Damascus, what happens a little before their arrival in that city?

Luke gives two more accounts in the book of Acts: in reporting Paul's sermon (from then on, Saul was called only by his Roman name Paul) before his imprisonment in Jerusalem (22:6-21) and in reporting Paul's speech before Agrippa, when he was a captive in Caesarea (26:9-18).

A blinding light and a voice: "Saul, Saul . . ." Saul knows that the God whom he serves sometimes calls individuals by name. This was true of Abraham and of many others in the history of his people. When he was a child Samuel had to learn that God had spoken to him (1 Samuel 3). But God has no name; God is *Yahweh:* "I am who I am" or "I will be who I will be" (Exodus 3:12-14).

Saul falls on his knees and hears a voice asking him a cryptic question: "Why do you persecute me?" The dialogue is brief but has a powerful impact:

"Who are you, Lord?"

"I am Jesus, whom you are persecuting."

To strike the disciples is to strike Christ. Jesus, in the parable of the last judgment, shows how far he identifies himself with the person who suffers: "*I* was hungry . . . *I* was a stranger . . . *I* was in prison" (Matthew 25:31-46, italics added).

The man who was on his way to wreak violence against Christians is stopped in his tracks by another violence—

God's. It is such a brutal shock to him that he is traumatized, and for several days he is blinded and can take no food.

No one can explain the facts that are reported. We have to assess the consequences they had in a man's whole life and in his many writings. On the road to Damascus God suddenly demolished the foundation under the whole dogmatic system that gave structure to Saul's Hebraic faith. It was also a deep wound in that it separated Saul from his friends.

Saul had the pride of the Pharisees (often denounced by Jesus), that of being a strict observer of the law, of carrying out its requirements, and of knowing its rewards. Here his pride receives a terrible slap. He is constrained to discover that he has completely deceived himself. While he considered himself righteous, zealous to do the will of God, he sees himself revealed as the persecutor of Jesus-Messiah.

God does not let him founder in despair but picks him up and orders him to go into the city where he will learn what he ought to do. Peter, the repentant renegade, had also been confirmed in his ministry as an apostle by the living Christ. In whatever way it happens the servants of Christ across the centuries will have to see themselves broken in order to become readied for his service.

On the strength of the exceptional experience that took place on the Damascus road we cannot say that Saul had been making his way toward the Christian faith. It is a brutal revolution that puts him immediately at the service of the One whom he was persecuting and whose "slave" he will thenceforth claim to be.

In the course of his missionary life and through his writings Paul's strong personality is etched on our minds.

We discover the firmness of his character, his live sensitivity, his authority, and his gifts of persuasion. We discover his prophetic way of interpreting the unfolding pageant of history. We realize his concrete concern for the local churches. Finally, we see the way he uses his Hebrew upbringing and his Greek culture. In all these we can discern the lines of his vocation, which left their imprint on his spirituality.

It was the living Jesus who suddenly came into Saul's life in an unforeseen and compelling way. Saul had been struggling against a humiliated Messiah, conquered, agonizing between two thieves on a cross. Lo and behold the Suffering Servant is the true Christ, the One whom God glorifies. This discovery, like a flash of lightning, illuminates so many wonderful pages on the cross, which we read in Paul's letters to the different churches.

To the churches in Galatia, he could assert: "Far be it from me to glory except in the cross of our Lord Jesus Christ [Gal. 6:14]."

In his first letter to the Corinthians Paul teaches: "For the word of the cross is folly to those who are perishing, but to us who are being saved it is the power of God" (1 Corinthians 1:18-25).

In Paul's letter to the Colossians we can read a hymn to Christ: "For it pleased God to reconcile all things by Him and for Him . . . having established peace by the blood of His cross" (Colossians 1:15-22, TOB).

This glorified Christ who blocks the road for Saul will remain for him the near Jesus, the abiding presence, with whom he has a great intimacy: "It is no longer I who live, but Christ who lives in me [Gal. 2:20]." Paul speaks of it only with reticence in his letters to the churches. But this profound communion can be guessed behind everything we know of him.

His whole teaching and his sermons recall the unmerited grace of God that takes away all our pride, the grace Saul has discovered so suddenly and violently.

Picked up at once, Saul arrives at Damascus, spends several days with the disciples, receives baptism by one of them, and proclaims in the synagogues Jesus the Son of God. But he experiences at once the distrust of the believers in Damascus, as in Jerusalem. The Christians in the Jewish capital cannot bring themselves to believe that Saul has been converted. At the same time he experiences the suffering of being rejected by members of his own people, who want to kill him.

The split between Saul and his former Jewish brothers goes with him all his life. He must have experienced this division more intensely than others. In his teaching he calls up, in a majestic fresco, the salvation that Israel, after the gentiles, will find in Christ (Romans 11:25ff.) and proclaims that the two peoples will thereby be made one.

We cannot but marvel as we see how God chooses this thirteenth apostle, who was needed so that the gospel could be proclaimed to the Mediterranean world.

XV

Peter's Horizon Enlarged

(ACTS 9:32—10:48)

Every one who believes in him receives forgiveness of sins through his name [10:43].

Even though he wanted to stay in Jerusalem, Peter had to leave the capital and take to the Roman roads. Luke notes his passage to Lydda, a center of rabbinic culture. There he performs a miracle and opens hearts to the message of the gospel.

He is called to Joppa, another Jewish city that served as a port for Jerusalem. There a disciple lay dying. To paint the portrait of this dying woman with the beautiful name, Tabitha (which means gazelle), he writes: "She was full of good works and acts of charity [9:36]." Tabitha must have had a personality and a faith whose radiance went beyond the walls of her house, because her return to life was known by the whole city and prompted Peter to remain a long time in Joppa.

Peter had not yet encountered a pagan city of real importance. It would seem that, without assessing the meaning of this choice, the apostles had obeyed God's strategy in sending them into the urban centers.

Thus by unexpected means Peter is led to Caesarea. This Mediterranean port was the metropolis of Palestine. The Roman procurators preferred to live there rather than in Jerusalem. The city, proud of its massive stone breakwater and its amphitheater that could seat twenty thousand, was the headquarters of a Roman garrison.

Among the centurions the commander of the Italian Cohort, named Cornelius, was a remarkable man. Luke notes, in Acts as in his Gospel, Roman captains who attracted the friendship of the Jews whose country they were occupying. Such was the case of the centurion of Capernaum (Luke 7:1-10), of the one on duty at Golgotha (Luke 23:47), and of those who were assigned to guard Paul (Acts 27:1, 3, 43).

Such an officer, whose generosity and piety Luke underlines, could have been acquainted with the religious movements that had stirred Jerusalem and could have gathered some information about their leaders.

One fact is important for us: Cornelius, as he prays, receives from God as the answer to his spiritual search the message that he must listen to a certain Simon, named Peter, in Joppa. He immediately dispatches two of his house servants and a soldier to go and meet Peter.

Let us admire the promptness of his decision. He does

not make any pretext of the press of military duties to give him an excuse for postponing the consideration of essential questions.

God prepares the apostle to receive the messengers who are going to knock at his door and does it in a way that surprises our modern minds. We find it hard to make any sense of the strange vision that comes to Peter during his siesta in the midday heat. No psychoanalyst is there to give us the explanation we would like to have. We can guess that Peter was unconsciously in mental torment because of all the Jewish ritual rules concerning food, about which we read in the eleventh chapter of Leviticus.

Three times during his perplexity Peter heard what he took to be a divine voice. Three times the voice said, "What God has cleansed, you must not call common [10:15]," reinforcing the teaching of his Master. But the apostle had not yet pushed the consequences of the gospel to the limit in order to translate them into the concrete situation of his daily life and of his witness. Is it not often thus in our churches? Then why should we be surprised to find it so in this instance?

God has different teaching methods for each one of us. With Saul, the passionate man, God uses a certain violence. But with Peter, God uses patience to prod him along the path of his spiritual discoveries. I might even say that here God is laying a snare for Peter.

Inspired by the Spirit, the apostle welcomes the envoys of Cornelius. The next day he goes with them to Caesarea. He enters the Roman soldier's house and finds himself in the presence of the members of his family and his friends. Peter lifts up the centurion, who is kneeling at his feet. In so doing he says simply, "I too am a man [10:26]." This is a word that sets Peter off from all the priests and all the Caesars of that time—a word that should remain the watchword of all ministers of Jesus Christ.

The text allows us to imagine Peter's bewilderment when he finds himself in the house of a non-Jew. He expresses his embarrassment: "As you know, it is a crime for a Jew to have even the slightest contact with a foreigner [10:28, TOB]." But here he is, a Jew, looking at all these pagans who have sent for him in order to hear him.

We know church members whose racial prejudices make them blind or mean without their realizing it. Here we are thinking about Peter. He cannot hide the fact that the Jewish regulations are still very much on his mind. But can he refrain from proclaiming Jesus Savior to these people whose spiritual expectation he sees right before his eyes? This is God's snare for Peter.

To the Jews, at the first Pentecost, Peter had heralded the Messiahship of Jesus Christ and had called his hearers to repentance. Here, at the gathering in the house of the Roman officer, he does not quote scripture at length. The gentiles do not know these writings. Peter asserts that in every nation whoever fears God and practices justice finds a welcome with God (10:35).

Israel, the chosen people, can no longer be the one to dominate all the nations; it is to be the bearer of the message of the gospel, that of peace through Jesus Christ, through him "who is the Lord of all [10:36, TOB]."

How should we witness to our faith and proclaim the gospel? These questions raised by our contemporaries have also been pondered since the first years of the life of the church. Disciples have certainly agonized over them. Only the discernment that comes with receiving the Spirit can help men and women answer these questions.

Thus very early there was diversity in the ways the gospel was preached. Yet it was the same apostle preaching the same gospel. This is a point we must underline. We have seen, and we still see today, sectarian spirits imposing on succeeding generations or on other peoples, forms identical to the ones in which the good news of Jesus Christ has been transmitted to them.

Caesarea, therefore, is an important stage on Peter's course; it is his first contact with the Mediterranean world. In leading Peter there, God took him somewhat by surprise. Then, when God gave the Holy Spirit to pagans, God forcibly widened the horizon Peter saw—the horizon toward which the Savior is going to lead his messengers.

XVI

The New Name of "Christians"

(ACTS 11:19-30)

It is at Antioch that, for the first time, the name of "Christians" was given to the disciples [11:26, TOB].

When the disciples, driven out of Jerusalem, took refuge in Antioch they could hardly guess that this city would become the first religious capital of the Eastern church.

"Antioch, the beautiful"—for so it was called—was a large city that had become the prefecture of the province of Syria. It had rich buildings, powerful fortifications, but its inhabitants had the reputation of being morally depraved.

Today only the historians remember the evil reputation of the residents of this city, while the name of Antioch evokes for us the reputation of an almost model church.

What are the characteristics of this community that still make it an example?

Those who took refuge there because of their faith found a large number of synagogues. This was because Seleucus I, founder of the city in the third century B.C., had attracted many Jews to ensure its being well populated.

Welcomed by these Jews of Antioch, the disciples proclaim Jesus as Savior during the synagogue services. Luke does not register any opposition to this preaching; on the contrary, he notes many conversions.

When other refugees, natives of Cyprus and Cyrene, join them the nascent church also proclaims the good news of Christ to the Greeks. These things seem to be done spontaneously.

In this capital of a Roman province, with its port (Seleucia) six miles away on the Mediterranean, the various ethnic groups rubbed elbows a great deal. Jews and Greeks were neighbors. The former would have been less tradition-bound than their counterparts in Jerusalem.

Among these believers who had taken refuge in Antioch, no chief is specifically identified who might have led the assembly into taking great initiatives. Furthermore, the text makes no allusion to any plenary assembly in the course of which it might have been decided to bring the good news to the Greeks.

These are humble believers, open with one accord to the inspirations of the Spirit and willing to follow its guidance. The rank and file calmly confronted the "pillars of the church" with a fait accompli. To emphasize this is important.

Because of this inclusion of Greeks, the inhabitants of

Antioch no longer considered this church as simply another Jewish sect. Something was different about these people—something even an outsider could observe. Antioch citizens called them "Christians," as partisans of a certain "Christos."[1]

Perhaps these Christians have not suspected all that was revolutionary in the makeup of their church. But when news of the Antioch church reached Jerusalem the apostles and elders decided to send one of their number to investigate the real situation of this community. It is Barnabas who is chosen.

Joseph, the son of Levi, bore the appealing surname of Barnabas ("son of exhortation" or "preacher"). A man full of faith, generous, he had sold his field to bring the proceeds of its sale to the apostles (4:37). An open spirit, he is the person who is needed in such circumstances.

Recognizing how much the grace of God is at work in this Antioch church, he rejoices. Once again Luke notes this joy, a joy brought about by the discovery of unforeseen progress for the gospel.

Barnabas, by a wise inspiration, goes to seek Saul in Tarsus, where the brothers have sent him because the Jews were seeking to put him to death in Jerusalem. For a year Paul and Barnabas preach, teach, and edify the church of God in Antioch.

It is an admirable church, where the rashness of some inspired members is not criticized but understood and shared without any internal conflicts worth noting. Thus Greeks who have become Christians accept the teaching of two Jewish personalities, from elsewhere, who become for a short time their guides on the road of faith.

This Antioch church receives equally well some prophets who have come to it from Jerusalem.

The word may cause some confusion. The "prophets" were not soothsayers but people inspired by the Spirit of God, who saw things before others (often because they had a perceptive view of the present, which is preparing the future). Viewing this present, they publicly declared a judgment on it.

With the New Testament a new phase of prophecy begins. In his sermon at the temple Peter had said, "You are the sons of the prophets [3:25]." This, in the new covenant, is the fulfillment of what had been foretold by the prophet Joel. The daughters of Philip, one of the seven, will also prophesy (21:9).

Not only are the Jerusalem prophets welcomed, but they are also heard. One of them, Agabus, must have had special gifts, because he is named in this chapter and in another (21:10). He speaks of the coming famine. Luke has not been able to reconstitute the terms of his speech.

At that period famines occurred frequently. They were chronic scourges. Those who ate their fill must have become used to these situations. We too, we must admit, grow accustomed to the misery of the third and fourth worlds of today. This inspired emissary must have spoken of the hunger of those who are constantly victims of famine. He touched the hearts of the Christians in Antioch. And the Antioch church took an offering for the brothers and sisters in Judea, whose economic situation was grievous.

Two facts need to be considered: These prophet-preachers show themselves as persons sensitive to the distress of others and called to make this distress known to all. In one of his epistles Paul recalls forcefully: "If I have prophetic powers . . . but have not love, I am nothing [1 Cor. 13:2]." The love Christ inspires, extends for each one of us well beyond those who live under our gaze, beyond the limits of our city.

Furthermore, these gifts are offered by the Antioch church to the first Christian community gathered by the Lord Jesus, the one that could claim precedence as being "the mother church."

Yes, Barnabas had clearly recognized that the grace of God was at work when he saw in the Antioch church the effective service and witness of all, the abolition of any racial barrier between Jews and Greeks, the sense of Christian unity made clear by links of spiritual and material communion maintained with other churches.[2]

God is always in our present. "Jesus Christ is the same yesterday and today and for ever [Heb. 13:8]." So says the letter to the Hebrews, which tradition sometimes attributes to Barnabas. Can we rejoice to recognize these same marks of the authentic church in the Christian community of which we are members?

XVII

The First Overseas Mission

(ACTS 12:1—13:5)

While they were worshiping the Lord and fasting, the Holy Spirit said, "Set apart for me Barnabas and Saul for the work to which I have called them" [*13:2*].

The Jerusalem community experiences a new wave of persecutions. James, the brother of John, is put to death. Herod has Peter arrested but again God sets Peter free by secret means. The rescued apostle has time only to find a friendly house, to warn those gathered together, and then to plunge into the night to escape the searches of Herod's police. Thus Peter goes underground, and we lose track of him for some time.

How could the churches maintain themselves and grow after the disappearance—temporary or final—of two apostles and while surrounded by signs of hostility from so many powerful Jews? At the beginning the Roman army seemed indifferent, even though several centurions—and later on even a proconsul—became Christians (10:48; 13:12). This attitude did not last long.

Factors that made for the spread of the Christian faith have been identified by historians.[1] But we must not overlook an inexplicable factor: the power of the Holy Spirit to accomplish God's designs.

We modern Christians cannot help being struck by the vitality of these communities in the midst of persecutions. They outline for us the specific and essential characteristics of the church that remain constant in every period.

These strong units are bound up in a larger unity from the beginning. We are immediately astonished by the journeys undertaken by some members of these churches to visit others. We have seen Peter and John coming into Samaria, then going back to Jerusalem. We have seen Peter visiting Lydda, Joppa. Barnabas goes from the capital to Antioch; he goes to find Saul in Tarsus and brings him back to Antioch; then both of them take the relief offering to Jerusalem.

Doubtless using the roads laid out by Rome or the trading routes of the past and the present, these messengers of the Lord had neither the force of arms possessed by the Romans nor the power of money possessed by the traders. It is hard for us to conceive the dangers and difficulties that beset travelers in those days.

The faces of these visitors shortened the distance to the communities from which they came. The salutations that conclude certain letters echo the ties of a living family-type love. Thus Luke never had in mind any abstract or dogmatic notion of church when he referred to the congregations as a whole (9:31; 20:28).

The populations dominated by Rome probably had an idea of what centralization could be, with a visible capital—the administrative headquarters from which all orders came down. But as we perceive through the Acts, if the churches can sense their unity, it is because they have the same foundation, the same *invisible* Leader, the Lord Jesus.

The gentiles of Antioch have rightly chosen to designate the members of these communities by the name of the One to whom they belonged: Jesus Christ. And since that time they have been called Christians.

More important than the ties woven between these communities, it seems to me, is the tested solidity of each one. No doubt each congregation had a fringe of waverers around it—men and women with their weaknesses, their backslidings, and their denials. But each of these churches also had a group of responsible men and women as their leaders. These persons are often called elders, a word borrowed from the Jewish organization. The word elder calls to mind experience and wisdom as well as age. The Jerusalem church had its elders, to whom Barnabas and Saul turned over the offering from Antioch; the churches of Asia Minor will also have their elders.

Quite as often these leaders are called prophets or designated teachers. This diversity in the names given is an index of the respective gifts these persons brought to their leadership. We do not know whether they were chosen for a term or for life. Nor do we know whether they received a salary in order to devote their full time and energy to this charge. There must have been great variety in their leadership. But at every point their authority is exerted in a collegial way.

With many vivid touches Luke paints for us the fresco of these different churches. He shows us a supple organization, one the Holy Spirit could use and that would not block its inspirations.

Once again Antioch church leaders show us a magnificent witness to their firmness in the faith and their supple obedience to the orders of the Holy Spirit.

Fervently celebrating the Lord's Supper (the eucharist), the prophets and designated teachers (some of them mentioned by name) perceive clearly that the Holy Spirit is commanding them to set Saul and Barnabas apart for a special mission. What that mission is to be is not yet specified.

Until this time it was persecution that has obliged the Christians to leave for unknown cities and countries. Here it is obedience to an order of God that sends two church leaders on their way.

Antioch, then, was willing to do without the labor and the gifts of Barnabas and Saul because the Holy Spirit needed them elsewhere. This "elsewhere" is still vague. The departing travelers know that faith is a journey whose itinerary God only illumines little by little.[2] Since Damascus, Saul has learned that God may have some great surprise in store at a turning of the road. Much as we admire Saul, we must admire the Antioch church more. From the human standpoint it is that church which sends out the mission. It is that congregation whose faith is so open to the world that it can watch the wind fill the sails of the boat which is taking their leaders away from the seaport of Seleucia.

Before their departure there was what we would call a retreat, a day of prayer and fasting. Hands are laid on Barnabas and Saul. Not only the apostles have the privilege of laying on hands; in another circumstance Ananias had already laid his hands on Saul's head (9:17). John Mark accompanies them as their assistant. They turn first toward Cyprus, which is Barnabas' home country.

Luke's notice of their departure is compact: "They laid their hands on them and sent them off. So, being sent out by the Holy Spirit, they went down to Seleucia; and from there they sailed to Cyprus [13:3-4]."

Could anyone guess that such a quiet embarkation as a trip from Seleucia to Salamis (about one hundred fifty miles) would be the beginning of an epic of faith that is still carried forward today? How many of us are in sympathetic and supportive touch with the modern successors to Paul and Barnabas?

XVIII

A Door Opened to the Gentiles

(ACTS 13:13—14:28)

They gathered the church together and declared all that God had done with them, and how he had opened a door of faith to the Gentiles [*14:27*].

Paul's strong personality comes to the fore at the beginning of the journey. From this point on, Luke will mention his name first and call him by his Roman surname, "Paul."

Was Paul sure at this moment that God had set him apart to proclaim good news to the gentiles? When he picked himself up on the road to Damascus all he understood was that he would be told what to do (9:6). It is Ananias who, according to Luke, had learned that this former persecutor of Christians had been chosen to "carry [God's] name before the Gentiles and kings [9:15]." Only through Ananias does Paul learn how to interpret the overwhelming experience that has shaken him so. Here God is, rather surprisingly, entrusting to another person the meaning of a call to the inmost heart. In passing, let us note the tact of Ananias. (He left it to God to disclose the suffering in store for Paul [9:16].)

On the island of Cyprus, as they will do in Asia Minor, the messengers of God begin by visiting the synagogues in order to proclaim Jesus as Messiah. This is what they do at Salamis, at Paphos. In this latter city they have the joy of meeting a Roman proconsul who wishes to hear the Word of God and who "becomes a believer." For Paul, it may appear as an augury and a summons, confirming his call.

Luke spells out at greater length the ministry of the two envoys at Antioch-in-Pisidia, this city of the high plateau region where a large Jewish colony lived.

The missionaries go to the synagogue on the sabbath day. After the reading of the law and the prophets the rulers of the synagogue invite them: "If you have any word of exhortation for the people, say it [13:15]." There Paul proclaims Christ dead and risen and affirms that through Jesus we have this forgiveness and this justification that "you were not able to find in the law of Moses [13:38, TOB]."

This message was well received. Jews and proselytes alike asked for interviews with Paul and Barnabas. "The next sabbath almost the whole city gathered together to hear the word of God [13:44]." For this reason on that same day the hostility of the Jews broke out in aggression and violence.

Then the author of Acts tells us: "Paul and Barnabas spoke out boldly, saying, 'It was necessary that the word of God should be spoken first to you. Since you thrust it from you, and judge yourselves unworthy of eternal life, behold, we turn to the Gentiles' [13:46]."

Here is the public proclamation that finally and precisely defines the special mission of Paul and Barnabas. Note that John Mark is no longer present. He has left his companions on reaching the shore of Asia Minor at Perga (13:13).

After Paul and Barnabas make the solemn declaration they are driven from Antioch-in-Pisidia because the Jews have stirred up against them "the devout women of high standing and the leading men of the city [13:50]." The disciples, however, remain "filled with joy and with the Holy Spirit [13:52]."

The missionaries arrive at Iconium, where, Luke tells us, the same thing happens. They remain in this city for a long time, despite the opposition of the Jews, who rally some gentiles to their point of view. Paul and Barnabas are obliged to take refuge in Lystra and its surrounding area to avoid being stoned.

At Lystra, where they heal a cripple, they discover the bewilderment of the gentiles, who take Paul for Hermes and Barnabas for Zeus. But the hostility of the Jews pursues them. A group coming from Antioch-in-Pisidia and Iconium whips up the fury of the crowds. Paul is dragged outside the city, stoned, and left for dead. Rescued by the disciples, he picks himself up and with his faithful companion leaves for Derbe, where he proclaims the good news.

In the course of this first journey Paul and Barnabas see a profound modification in the human geography that is familiar to them. Up until that time their world had been divided into two groups: Jews and gentiles (Romans, Greeks, etc.). Christian preaching creates a new cleavage. Henceforth they will only know a single line of division. On the one side stand the Christians, whether of Jewish or gentile origin. The Antioch church has already sketched for them the picture of such a unity. Over against the combined Christian forces are the opponents of Christ, who can also be of Jewish or gentile origin.

This new alignment topples their whole world view. It is hard for us to imagine how profoundly shaken these ambassadors were. They were surely torn when they saw their Jewish brothers allying themselves with gentiles to pursue them and put them to death. We find the echo of this in the exhortations the apostles (for so Luke calls them now) give to the churches when they pay a second visit before returning to Antioch-in-Syria.

Along with exhortation these new communities need organization. The apostles have seen this new people of God gathered by the Holy Spirit and in response to their preaching. Now they take care to designate elders in each church, so that this solid nucleus may help the young churches to persevere. The apostles also warn these freshly converted Christians that "through many tribulations we must enter the kingdom of God [14:22]." Jesus had taught it; the missionaries had learned it by heart and in their flesh.

Did they remember Psalm 2, which had cast some light on their ordeal after the first arrest of Peter and John? The "kings of the earth" drawn up "against the Lord" then bore the names of Pilate and Herod. Today also forces oppose God's anointed—not kings but angry mobs with stones in their hands.

Luke hastens to describe the joy the messengers felt on returning to Antioch-in-Syria. Before the assembled church Paul and Barnabas give an account of their mission. Here again the author of Acts gives us only a short résumé of the essentials, because he has just told us the story of the journey. We do not know whether Paul spoke of the sufferings they endured. Later, when he writes his second letter to the Corinthians, he enumerates an impressive number of sufferings for Christ: "Five times I have received at the hands of the Jews the forty lashes less one. Three times I have been beaten with rods; once was I stoned [2 Cor. 11:24-25]."

The important thing is to let the Christians of Antioch know "all that God had done with them." Paul and Barnabas are eager to convey the joy their new disciples are experiencing, despite all their difficulties. This is the joy Luke so often notes. That joy is heightened by the momentous announcement the missionaries bring: "[God] had opened a door of faith to the Gentiles [14:27]."

On the local level the Christians of Antioch-in-Syria had experienced the opening of such a door. Paul and Barnabas were bringing them a certainty that was verified by a rich experience. It was a clear confirmation of the will of God.

For his part Peter, also outside Jerusalem, had been forced to bend before the will of God, despite the amazement of "the believers from among the circumcised [10:45]" when Peter had seen that the gentiles also were receiving the Spirit.

This experience and conviction had come to two apostles, Peter and Paul, in two different places, both beyond the reach of the original church in Jerusalem. Was this enough to clarify the question (i.e., the admission of gentiles as full-fledged Christians) for all the churches?

XIX

The Jerusalem Assembly

(ACTS 15:1-36)

Then why do you now provoke God by laying on the shoulders of these converts a yoke which neither we nor our fathers were able to bear? [*15:10,* NEB].

For some it was a matter of great joy that the door of the church had been opened to the gentiles. But a certain number of Jews who had become Christians (I shall call them "Judaizers") could not allow this door to stand wide open. According to this view, pagans should first pass through a kind of sieve, performing certain Jewish rites before they could penetrate the door of the church; gentiles must first be Jews, the males undergoing circumcision, before they could become Christians. Circumcision was considered necessary for salvation.

This is what some Judean Jews had been saying in Antioch-in-Syria—the same persons, or their fellow disciples of the same tendency, who had already gone up to Jerusalem to reproach Peter in the matter of his attitude toward gentiles who had become Christians (11:1-18). Perhaps the apostle had then convinced them that the message of Christ is addressed to all people. They had, Luke writes, "regained their calm, while giving glory to God [11:18, TOB]."

As we have seen, the church of Antioch-in-Syria had already made itself a center of controversy because it gathered together Greeks and Jews who had become Christians. The Jerusalem church had sent Barnabas to investigate the situation. He was fully convinced when he "saw the grace of God [11:23]" at work.

We can guess that the Judaizers ran into strong opposition in the Antioch church. The subject under discussion was grave. It concerned the increasing number of Christians who had come over from paganism, a number that was bound to grow if the missionary journeys continued.

This is why it is decided that Paul, Barnabas, and some others will go up to Jerusalem to explore this serious difference with the elders of the original church. A detail shows how strongly the Antioch church insisted that this question be clarified: The church itself pays the traveling expenses of its delegates (15:3).

Thus it is in Jerusalem that the two conceptions, and thus the two procedures for admitting pagans to the church, are brought face to face again.

The Judaizers came from Pharisaic circles. Saul of Tarsus had been one of their number. This group maintained that before they could be Christians all pagan adherents must be circumcised and obey the laws of Moses.

The discussion was serious and difficult. We do not know how long it lasted. It seems that first the apostles and the elders studied it among themselves. Then it was brought to the knowledge of the whole assembly of the church. There the Christians of pagan origin had no majority, because no representatives were present from the churches in Paphos, Antioch-in-Pisidia, Lystra, or Iconium. But some delegates from Antioch-in-Syria were there, as we have seen. Thus we cannot properly speak of a council or of a synod. We should content ourselves with calling it a "Jerusalem Assembly" that proved to be decisive for the future of the church.

As in all deliberative assemblies, it is the "stars" who speak. Peter takes the floor first. He states what he had already told the Judaizers who had come to take him to task. No longer is the *principle* of admitting gentiles into the church at issue; now it is the *means.* Is it necessary for the church to impose on Christians coming over from paganism the observance of Jewish practices—particularly circumcision?

"No!" says Peter. The sentence with which the apostle concludes must have had the effect of a thunderclap: "Once more, it is by the grace of the Lord Jesus, we believe, that we have been saved, exactly like them" (15:11 TOB)."

Luke notes that there was silence in the assembly after this speech. Paul and Barnabas then testify to the experiences that occurred during the missionary journey in Asia Minor. A stunned assembly listens.

James, who had become a "pillar of the church" in Jerusalem during Peter's absence, rises to suggest a compromise. He grants the principle of not imposing the obstacle of circumcision on gentile Christians. He suggests, however, that the converts should be asked only to respect certain Jewish prohibitions.

He proposes, and it is accepted, that they write these decisions in a letter and have the missive brought to Antioch-in-Pisidia by Paul, Barnabas, and other "leading men among the brethren [15:22]."

The letter presents those decisions as having been inspired by the Holy Spirit. The church in Antioch-in-Syria receives it with a sense of relief. Thus the schism which threatened to arise between the churches is avoided.

But a decision, no matter how important, must above all be lived. We learn from Paul's letters that the Judaizers resumed their old mentality from time to time. Why should that surprise us? We know the ever-present drawing power of "meritorious acts" or reassuring legalistic ceremonies when our devotion grows tepid. With what vigor and apostolic zeal Paul asks the Galatians: "How can you turn back again to the weak and beggarly elemental spirits? [Gal. 4:9]." The Galatians he is addressing are the members of the churches he and Barnabas had founded on their first journey. He states again: "For you were called to freedom [Gal. 5:13]."

After the fifteenth chapter no more mention is made of the apostle Peter. The second part of Acts tells us of Paul's different missions, which are all the more vivid in the telling, because Luke, often Paul's companion, is writing his personal memories at the same time. (These are the "we" passages.)

The last chapter leaves Paul in Rome. At the close of his third journey he had appealed his judgment to the Roman courts, because he was a Roman citizen. He stayed in Rome for two years as a prisoner, guarded by a soldier yet living in a private home at his own expense. Like Peter, who came to join him (if the tradition is to be credited), he must have died during the Neronian persecution.

Are the questions and trials of the church at its beginnings so far from us?

First, we must note that not all Jews became Christians during the first centuries. Once persecutors of the Christians, the Jewish people have, for centuries, become the persecuted in different countries and in different ways. Thus we cannot deal with Judeo-Christian relations only in terms of the past.

Escaped from the Holocaust, a minority of those who are attached to the Jewish tradition and faith live in our country, of which they are citizens with the same rights as ourselves. They are our contemporaries. We meet them or we know them.

When successive waves of anti-Semitism break around us do we react as the scriptures would inspire us to do? Do we remember that Jesus of Nazareth was a Jew?

When the church today proclaims the gospel to other continents is it with the freedom the Spirit gives, without imposing Western thought forms or life-styles on the people who are welcoming the good news of the realm of God?

Finally, there is in every community an inclusive tendency and an opposite exclusive tendency. The people of the new covenant are divided on the subject of who should enter it. In facing this issue we may learn from the Jerusalem church. The first church was willing to acknowledge that it was not the sole proprietor of the Holy Spirit. We still run the danger that, like the Judaizers, we may forget that Jesus is the Lord of all.

There is also the risk that we, coming from gentile backgrounds as we do, may forget the Jewish roots of our faith. The Jerusalem church, humbled by the proofs of the work of the Holy Spirit away from its own bosom, knew how to avoid a schism between the two churches. It may be that the church at its beginnings has a final lesson to give to divided Christians: "There is neither Jew nor Greek, there is neither slave nor free, there is neither male nor female; for you are all one in Christ Jesus [Gal. 3:28]."

NOTES

II. Peter Fills Out the Twelve

1. This reference to a guillotine that falls on the fervor of an authentic vocation is autobiographical. Elisabeth Schmidt experienced a call to the Christian ministry at a Student Christian Movement retreat in the early thirties, took top honors at the Geneva Protestant Seminary, and was sent to revive a marginal parish in the Cévennes mountains. Normally, she would have been ordained after a year's probationary service. Because she was a woman she spent fourteen years in the most difficult of parishes, performing all the functions of a pastor with the status of a licentiate, to the deep satisfaction of her parishioners and the tacit approval of the church authorities. Finally, the official board of the parish where she had endured the German and American occupations of World War II prevailed on the National Synod of the French Reformed Church to ordain her on October 29, 1949. She was the first woman to be ordained in the French Reformed Church, the largest Protestant church in France. The story of her good-tempered endurance is movingly told in her autobiography, *When God Calls a Woman: The Struggle of a Woman Pastor in France and Algeria* (New York: The Pilgrim Press, 1981).

VI. *The Song of This Joy*

1. The French word is *allégresse,* suggesting a lively tempo in music. Robert Louis Stevenson strikes the same note when he prays, "Give us to *go blithely* on our business all this day" (from prayer "At Morning," in *Prayers Written at Vailima* [London: Chatto & Windus, 1910], italics added).

IX. *The Community at Prayer*

1. The words of the psalm in question are:

Why do the nations conspire,
  and the peoples plot in vain?
The kings of the earth set themselves,
  and the rulers take counsel together,
  against the Lord and his anointed.
—Psalm 2:1-2

X. *Prison, Deliverance, and Rods*

1. Elisabeth Schmidt has taken her own share of "suffering for Christ." Her book *When God Calls a Woman* describes matter-of-factly her service at the concentration camp in Gurs, where she was stricken with typhoid; her night of emergency nursing in Sète, where American planes had inflicted fifty-two casualties on the German-held port city; her going, without sleep, to intercede for a Protestant service for three of the victims and her participation in the mass funeral, which was tipped (apart from her participation) toward a political statement for Pétain.

She includes in her text a moving statement by a Protestant colleague, Pastor Roland de Pury, of Lyon, who had been imprisoned for his activities on behalf of the Jewish victims of Nazism. After his release Pastor de Pury wrote:

> Keep on praying as you have done until now. For there are all those who remain behind the closed door. There are all the prisoners in the world . . . and no one can imagine the despair which fills them. May God give you his own compassion, his infinite pity for the captives. We have to be free and to free every creature.
>
> —*When God Calls a Woman* by Elisabeth Schmidt, The Pilgrim Press, New York, 1981, page 83.

XVI. The New Name of "Christians"

1. The believers needed and got a new name *only when they had opened the door to seekers of another race and nation.*

2. This may explain why a modern city church might choose this name, as Antioch Baptist Church. Of the churches mentioned in the New Testament, what other city (except Rome, of course) has this distinction?

XVII. The First Overseas Mission

1. The reader may pause to identify some of these. Among those that come to mind are the moral decadence of some segments of the society, the indolence induced by dependence on slave labor, the split loyalties attendant on polytheism—all these problems required remedies. In the

opposite direction, Roman roads and peace, however stern it was; widespread use of Greek . . .

2. Here we find a striking resemblance to a passage in Elisabeth Schmidt's autobiography (*When God Calls a Woman,* op.cit.). She speaks, on page 20 of that book, of the advice given her by a seminary professor in Geneva. On her graduation he told her: "The Savior does not trace out the path for us in advance. He makes it clear to us from day to day."